Faith and Works

FAITH

AND

WORKS

*THE BUSINESS, POLITICS,
AND PHILANTHROPHY OF ALABAMA'S*
JIMMY FAULKNER

A BIOGRAPHY BY
ELVIN STANTON

NewSouth Books
Montgomery

NewSouth Books
P.O. Box 1588
Montgomery, AL 36102

ISBN 1-58838-092-0

Design by Randall Williams

Printed in the United States of America

Contents

Photos follow page 128.

Foreword

I have known Dr. Jimmy Faulkner for fifty-five years. There's not a more familiar name in the South than Jimmy Faulkner. He is a man of honor, integrity, and the highest type of humanity.

Jimmy has received many awards, accolades, and thousands of applauses, but I've never detected any conceit, egotism, or arrogance on his part. He has always been a very humble person.

The Greek philosopher, Diogenes, spent his life looking for an honest man. If it were possible for Diogenes to come to Bay Minette, Alabama, I think he would say, "I have found my man."

Jimmy in so many ways is an extraordinary person. When I think of him, I think of the lines of Shakespeare: "His life was gentle; and elements so mixed in him, that nature might stand up and say to all the world, 'This was a man.'"

Jimmy has spent his life helping others. There was a time when Faulkner University had some severe financial problems. I am convinced that if it had not been for Faulkner's concern and liberality for the school, there might not be a Faulkner University today. It is only fitting that the school should bear his name.

I am so thankful to have known a person who is so kind and liberal and who has for many years supported every good work to the best of his ability. In this book you will read of the amazing things Jimmy has accomplished in a short period of eighty-six years.

Dr. Faulkner is a great communicator. Aristotle's rhetoric teaches us that there are three things necessary to be a successful communicator:

1) "ethos"— the ability to talk to people in a way that they want to hear what you have to say. Dr. Faulkner has this ability.

2) "pathos" — the ability to speak in a way that the listeners believe the speaker cares for them. Dr. Faulkner's genuine desire to help people gives his listeners assurance of his concern.

3) "logos" — the ability to convince and persuade people. Jimmy Faulkner has been blessed with the great gifts that Aristotle says are so necessary to be a great communicator.

Dr. Faulkner is a good husband, good father, good grandfather, good citizen, and good Christian gentleman. I am proud to say he is a good friend of mine.

V. P. BLACK

Preface

The poem "I Am A Builder" (page 16) was a favorite of the late United States Senator James B. "Jim" Allen, and the beloved Alabama statesman would be the first to say that James Herman "Jimmy" Faulkner, Sr., is a true builder in every sense of the word.

Jim Allen knew Jimmy Faulkner well. After all, they served together in the state senate when Allen was lieutenant governor, they both ran for governor of Alabama in the same primary, and Allen would later credit Faulkner with his own election to the U.S. Senate.

While Faulkner has been a friend and confidant of presidents, governors, members of Congress and state legislators in numerous states, there is so much more to the life of this man than politics. An octogenarian with twice the energy of many two decades his junior, Faulkner is a tireless builder in his own community, in state and local education, and—more importantly to him—his church.

Jimmy and his older brother, Thurston, were born on a postage-stamp sized farm in rural Lamar County. Their father, Henry L. Faulkner, eked out a living from the red clay hills of west

11

Alabama and hoped to save enough money to help his sons get a solid education, something he had been denied. However, it was their mother, Ebbie, a schoolteacher, who saw that both boys got to school on time and tended to their studies. Both parents instilled into their boys the strong work ethic, a deep and abiding faith in God, and a desire and love for education that would serve them well in the years ahead. With Henry Faulkner's tragic death when Jimmy was only twelve years old, the heavy burden of family responsibility fell hard and suddenly upon the shoulders of the mother, who welcomed the consolation and assistance of her two young sons.

The faith and values that became the bedrock of his life, and the lessons he learned in childhood, followed Jimmy Faulkner in 1936 to Bay Minette, the courthouse-square town of sprawling live oaks in Baldwin County in southwest Alabama adjacent to Mobile. Bay Minette is the town that he and his family, with great affection, would thereafter call home.

Even now, Faulkner's travels may take him as far away as South America, searching for new industry, or perhaps to any of the eight cities which house offices of the company he serves as vice chairman. But Sunday mornings, as surely as the sun rises, will find him making the short drive from his spacious home, nestled in the stately tall pines on East Fifth Street, to the Bay Minette church of Christ. Church attendance is not optional for Faulkner. Religion is at the very center of his life and as a member of his church, he has always been a builder. He believes that the Bible is the word of God and provides the scriptural answer for all of life's questions. Whether as a Sunday School teacher or Elder, Faulkner has always been active in the church. But he also has strong convictions about stewardship, believing "you just cannot outgive God." Years ago Faulkner began designating not ten, but fifty percent of what he earned to the church, Christian education, and other good causes. Not only has he given of his own resources, he has raised millions for church of Christ educational institutions. Faulkner believes in putting his faith to work, and that one cannot serve God without serving others.

Jimmy Faulkner is a builder of his community and takes great joy in improving the quality of life of its people. Long before there was an industrial development board in Baldwin County, Faulkner was hard at work bringing new industry and better jobs to the area. Now, after a half-century of unparalleled achievement, his local board has named him "Chairman Emeritus." With his unique blend of polite personal charm and bulldog tenacity, Faulkner has enjoyed uncanny success in hooking and landing for his community new industries as diverse as dental products and compressors.

Today, Baldwin County, largest in land area in the state, is one of the fastest growing areas in the Southeast and, with nearly two hundred new businesses each year, it is the second-fastest growing county in Alabama. Nestled between Mobile Bay on the west and the Gulf of Mexico on the south, Baldwin County is an increasingly popular billion-dollar resort area and tourist mecca. State and local development leaders agree that much of the growth can be attributed directly to Jimmy Faulkner.

Next to his church and his family, Faulkner's greatest love is education. He recognizes that education is the cornerstone of both personal success and community economic development. And Jimmy Faulkner is a builder in education. His hard work and devotion to education was recognized at the state level when he was appointed in 1978 to the Alabama Commission on Higher Education (ACHE). He later was elected its chairman. In 1982, the Alabama Association of Colleges and Universities honored him for his "exemplary dedication" to higher education.

Faulkner has also worked hard for education locally. He was named chairman of the Public Education Building Commission of Bay Minette in 1967 and was highly influential in locating a state community college in his home town. In 1971, Bay Minette residents convinced the governor to rename the school the James H. Faulkner Junior College. In addition, he has been a financial supporter of Freed-Hardeman College, a church of Christ junior college in Tennessee where he began his higher education journey. But for the past forty years, Faulkner has given sacrificially of his time, energy, and finances to a university formerly known as Alabama Christian College in Montgomery. In recognition and honor of his efforts, in 1983 the board of directors changed the name of the institution to Faulkner University. He thus became the only living man in Alabama, if not the nation, to have both a university and a community college named in his honor.

Jimmy Faulkner is a builder, a builder "who works with care, measuring life by the rule and square." Through his own life, he has built a monument that stands firmly on the sturdy pillars of his faith in God, his devotion to education, his dedication to his community, and his political leadership and counsel. The monument of his life speaks volumes more than the words of any book could ever express.

An African proverb states that when an elder dies, a library burns to the ground. I am deeply grateful to have visited and to have learned from one of Alabama's greatest libraries while it still stands, tall and vibrant on our landscape.

It is my sincere desire that others will benefit from this visit and be inspired, as I have been, to do more, to give more, to care more, and to become more than previously thought possible, because of the example of this erudite Alabamian.

ELVIN STANTON

Faith and Works

Am I A Builder?

I watched them tearing a building down,
A group of men in a busy town.
With a ho-heave-ho and lusty yell
They swung a beam, and the side wall fell.
I asked the foreman: "Are these men skilled,
And the men you'd hire if you had to build?"
He gave a laugh and said: "No, indeed!
Just common labor is all I need.
I can easily wreck in a day or two
What builders have taken a year to do."
And I thought to myself as I went away,
Which of these roles have I tried to play?
Am I a builder who works with care,
measuring life by the rule and square?
Am I shaping my deeds to a well-made plan,
Patiently doing the best I can?
Or am I a wrecker, who walks the town
Content with the labor of tearing down?

Author Unknown

Introduction

On an unseasonably warm January morning, a black limousine pulled up to the entrance to the modest hotel on the east side of Montgomery. The young woman driver slid from the front seat, clutched an official-looking clipboard, and walked up to the tall silver-haired, lanky, distinguished-looking man waiting outside.

"Are you Mr. Jimmy Faulkner?" she asked with a pleasant smile. When he nodded, she continued, "I'm your driver and I've been assigned to take you and your wife to the inauguration ceremonies, stay with you as long as you need me, and then bring you back."

Faulkner had not asked for this unusual treatment. He had simply told a state senator friend that he planned to attend the inauguration, as he had attended so many others in the past. The friend relayed the information to a member of the inaugural committee. Suddenly these extraordinary arrangements were in place for this icon of Alabama politics, including special seating on the very front row of the reserved section facing the speaker's stand.

This VIP treatment was not afforded because Faulkner had played a special role in the election of this particular governor, as he had for governors on other occasions. The honor simply was in keeping with Faulkner's esteem and prestige in Alabama politics.

Faulkner attended his first inauguration in 1939 when Frank Dixon became governor. At age twenty-two, Faulkner had served as Dixon's Baldwin County campaign manager. He has attended many inaugurations since.

Faulkner knows Alabama politics inside and out. He was voted outstanding freshman state senator before twice deciding to make the big race for governor. Thoughts of those races played through his mind as he and Karlene, his new wife of three years, sat in the back seat of the limousine on the way to the State Capitol. He could hardly believe forty-five years had passed since he was nosed out of a 1954 run-off with James E. "Big Jim" Folsom by just over 7,000 votes out of a total vote of nearly 600,000. Of course, Faulkner had handily carried his home county of Baldwin and his native county of Lamar, but he also beat Folsom in Jefferson, Alabama's most populous county. Faulkner would later discover that on election night, Folsom's campaign workers were able to "steal" more than enough votes to force Faulkner from the runoff. He would always believe that his own campaign naiveté and lack of poll-watchers allowed the election to slip from his fingers. Interestingly, the third man in the race was James B. (Jim) Allen, who would become a dear friend and later credit Faulkner with his own election to the United States Senate.

In 1958, Faulkner again ran for governor in a crowded Democratic primary field of fourteen candidates, including John Patterson and George Wallace. This time, Faulkner came in third as Patterson rode to victory on the huge tide of sympathy from the assassination of his Attorney General-elect father, who had been gunned down during the vice cleanup of Phenix City. The 1958 campaign was Faulkner's last try for governor, and it would be the only Alabama loss for Wallace, who later relied heavily on Faulkner for political counsel and financial support in five other races for governor and three for president.

But this was another day. And a beautiful, spring-like day it was, so unusual for a January inauguration, as the sun beamed down on the brightly colored floats and the succession of blaring high school bands that punctuated the long inaugural parade. Faulkner remembered earlier ceremonies when the temperature plunged into the teens, a strong, bone-chilling north wind whipped the bare legs of high school cheerleaders, and the band members could hardly play their instruments. Not today. On this January 1999 inaugural morning the sun was brightly smiling on this parade.

Another parade was also in progress, one almost unnoticed at the reviewing stand. Former mayors, county commissioners, state legislators, judges, attorneys, and long-time political activists had easily spotted Faulkner, towering above the crowd in his tan western felt hat. One and two at a time they made their way over to shake the hand of the polite but powerful Southern gentleman they had known for years. Faulkner soon abandoned his comfortable reserved seat to stand beside the rope that cordoned off the reviewing stand from the crowd so that he could reach out to his well-wishers. Some he recognized immediately as old friends. Others, after brief introductions, he would recall from campaigns or business relationships of many years ago. But all knew Jimmy Faulkner and were eager to pay homage to a man whose fingerprints were on so many political campaigns over most of the past century.

Shortly after noon, the Faulkners were ushered back into their reserved limousine by the attentive young lady who had stood by them throughout the ceremony. As they maneuvered through the traffic, Faulkner reflected on the inauguration of Governor Don Siegelman.

"A very unusual address," he offered. "Most inaugural speeches contain something for everybody to take home with them. Things like better highways, more industry and better jobs, better care for the elderly, improvements in schools and higher education, better health care, and help for the farmers. But this speech was a lot like his campaign speeches with emphasis on the lottery for education."

Faulkner's observation reflected the reality that while inaugural ceremonies have not changed so much over the years, political campaigning surely has. Gone are the days of setting up loudspeakers in front of county courthouses, blasting music from gospel quartets and country bands, and those highly charged, emotional speeches from candidates that stroked the heart strings of every important issue of concern to the local audience. Today's campaigns are extremely sophisticated, well-organized media campaigns that emphasize only those issues that have been identified, probed, and thoroughly tested by polling firms and focus groups. Though Faulkner was himself a pioneer in the use of opinion polls in earlier years, he expresses unease that polls now play such a determining role. Today's political polling is a highly refined science that dictates the entire focus of campaigns. Yesteryear's rambling campaign speeches have been replaced with carefully crafted soundbites. Candidates deflect reporters' questions to the issues that computer-driven polling has identified as most likely to result in election. This year, for winning candidate Don Siegelman, the issue was the lottery.

Faulkner knew that in years past no political candidate in his or her right mind would dare embrace any form of gambling in this deep-south, God-fearing, conservative state. But highly professional polling had identified the lottery as an acceptable alternative to higher taxes, provided it was tied to improving education and furnishing scholarships for families who otherwise might not be able to send their children to community colleges or universities. Against an opposing candidate who seemed to have no viable alternative to funding improvements for education, the state lottery issue elected this new governor who would lead Alabama into the twenty-first century.

Yes, it was a new day in Alabama politics. And through it all, Jimmy Faulkner had bridged the gap between two centuries. When elected to his first office in the early forties, he was only twenty-four and known as the youngest mayor in America. He won his state political stripes in the campaigns of the fifties and sixties, was sought out for his counsel and assistance during the seventies and eighties. And now, stepping into the new millennium, this astute octogenarian is one of the most respected political figures in the South. And still, he remains more active than many men decades his junior.

Over the years, holding political office has ceased to be a goal for Faulkner. Instead, he has mastered the art of using the political process for more meaningful achievements. This eminently successful businessman remains a friend and confidant of presidents, governors, members of congress and state legislators in numerous states. However, his main concern continues to be the plight of those less fortunate. He is deeply involved in improving the quality of life of the people of his community, his state and the nation. He is a firm believer that education is the stepladder to success and should be made available to every aspiring person. A man who once turned down an outright appointment to the United States Senate because of his deep loyalty to a deceased friend, he values personal friendships far more than earthly treasures and personal acclaim.

And on this particular inauguration day, many of his friends lined up to salute this smiling, distinguished godfather of Alabama politics.

As WE HAVE SEEN, family, church, education, community, politics, and industry are all facets of Faulkner's distinguished life. To really understand the charisma, integrity, humility, and the essence of this famous Alabamian, one must examine the roots of Jimmy Faulkner: roots that auger deep into the red clay hills of west Alabama.

1

Red Clay Roots

I n the late 1800s, before the turn of the century, the Georgia-Pacific Railroad was pushing its lines through the United States and the South and tracks were popping up like varicose veins in unexpected areas. Such was the case in sleepy Lamar County, Alabama, when the *Northern Alabama Historical and Biographical*, published in 1888, declared, "With the completion of this great line the county will be speedily appreciated and developed."

At that time, the county seat of Vernon boasted a population of only three hundred. This section of the state was far removed from any mass transportation and, therefore, placed at a great disadvantage, notwithstanding its rich stores of minerals. The Buttahatchie River, along with Weaver Creek, Coal Fire Creek, and Yellow Creek, snaked among some five hundred and fifty gravel-dirt hills and the fertile farmlands of Lamar County.

The population of some twelve thousand consisted of mainly farmers who tilled the red loam soil to produce cotton, corn, wheat, and oats. Nearly half of the cultivated land was devoted to cotton, and the county produced more than five thousand bales a year.

Plentiful native grasses provided for livestock.

It was in this setting that Jimmy Faulkner's grandparents, Wiley Polk Faulkner and Alabama Jane Hays Faulkner, built their small farmhouse and, with great hope and hard work, set out to make a living. It was an area that years earlier had been split by the War Between the States (Civil War) and Polk's father, Burrell Lanier Falkner, "sat out" the war and refused allegiance to either side. He later became the first Probate Judge of Lamar County.

Henry Lanier Faulkner, oldest son of Polk and "Bama" Faulkner, followed his parents' example and, as a teenager, was given his own small plot of farmland. After he proved his devotion to the long cotton rows, his father added a few more acres to his stewardship.

There were no tractors or automobiles back then, but Henry stashed away enough savings to buy a buggy to hitch to the horse. Soon, on Saturday nights, the buggy and Henry would bump down the long dirt road to Kingville, and to the home of a pretty brunette school teacher fondly known as "Miss Ebbie" Johnson.

On March 17, 1910, Henry, decked out in his only suit, and Ebbie, in her home-made wedding gown, were married at her home as close friends and family members gathered for the celebration. After the ceremony, the two made their home in a small farmhouse Henry had bought from his brother-in-law, Francis Varnon. They had two children, both boys. Thurston L. Faulkner was born December 2, 1911, and James Herman Faulkner was born March 1, 1916.

> If I were hanged on the highest hill,
> Mother o' Mine, O mother o' mine!
> I know whose love would follow me still,
> Mother o' mine, O mother o' mine!
>
> Rudyard Kipling

The opening stanza of English writer Rudyard Kipling's "Mother o' Mine" demonstrates the depth of a mother's love for her child. From his earliest days, snuggled in the warm and tender arms of his mother, young Jimmy was closely nurtured. He and his mother remained inseparable, especially after his father's life was snuffed out in a tragic, fiery accident.

"My daddy obviously loved my mother and they always got along fine. I never heard them say a cross word to each other. Mom was better educated, and finally got her college degree, and was loved by everybody. She taught school for thirty-nine years and had thousands of students who affectionately called her 'Miss Ebbie,' 'Cousin Ebbie,' and in some cases 'Aunt Ebbie.' She was a popular, efficient mathematics teacher and a great disciplinarian. She had the ability to look at you, talk to you and shame you into submission.

"I was born in March, and that summer and fall my mother not only cared for me, but she also picked three bales of cotton in the hot sun. When I was four, my mother was teaching school at Sunny Side, three miles away. Having nothing better to do with me, she started me to school at this early age. My older brother, Thurston, drove Bonnie, the mare, and we rode to school in a buggy each day.

"My daddy was a stern man with comparatively little education, but brilliant in common sense. People from miles around would come to him for advice on doctoring their animals and things of that nature. He worked hard, and expected everybody else to do the same, particularly his two sons. He had a temper which he sometimes let loose on Thurston and me, and I felt that he was kind of rough on Thurston. A couple of years before he died, Papa and I became very close and he seldom, if ever, reprimanded me. However, he was not hesitant to instruct me on how to do things, and corrected me if I did them wrong, but usually in a pleasant manner. Actually, he was a great father and I loved him dearly," Faulkner recalls.

It was not an easy childhood, growing up on a west Alabama dirt farm near the Mississippi state line, but one that did provide fond memories.

"I worked and played with my father, mother, older brother, the hired hand Hezzy Gilliam, and the neighboring boys and girls down on Yellow Creek in Lamar County. We thought we were overworked, but we probably were not. Papa showed me how to plow a mule when I was just eight years old. When I was ten, we had a Fordson tractor and he had me on it, going around and around plowing in the big fields," Faulkner remembers.

"I was proud of that tractor! It was one of the first in the community. It had fenders, two tanks, one that held three gallons of gasoline and the other about twelve gallons of kerosene. We used the gasoline to start and warm up the tractor, then switched to kerosene to use while plowing the fields. Papa would put me up on that tractor, and I would turn the beautiful earth with a turning plow. I was so proud that we were able to have such a huge implement. We had two disks we could mount on the side of the tractor that turned the soil instead of pulling one behind, like most of them did.

"Not all soil was the same and sometimes I would get back at the end of the field and hit a soft spot, and the tractor would stall and go dead. I was too small to crank it, so I would have to go get Papa. This always made him slightly angry because he would be working at something and didn't need to take time out to crank my tractor. But of course, he had to, and always did," Faulkner noted.

Even though the Faulkner farm boasted a new tractor, the mules were still used for plowing cotton and corn. In the smaller fields, the tractor would knock down too many stalks.

"We also used Pat and Minnie for such things as raking hay, pulling the wagon or the sleds, or plowing in the garden. They were a fine pair of mules and in the summer, when crops were laid by, and in the winter, Papa would use them to drag logs to the Interstate Railroad, which went through the back of our farm. They were purported to be the finest pair of mules in the county and, of course, I proudly thought so, even if they weren't," he boasted.

There was no end to the chores on a small rural farm in those days.

"We worked hard . . . milked the cows, fed the hogs, fed the mules and did all the things around the house and the farm, and we never got through working. When I was eleven, my mother taught school in Vernon. At that time we had a Model T, and I would sit on top of my book satchel to see over the steering wheel to drive the thirteen miles over dusty or muddy roads to school. After hard rains, we had to go south ten miles around Steens, Mississippi, back on to Columbus Pike to get to Vernon. It was a long trip of over forty miles and took us over two hours," Faulkner recalls.

LEISURE TIME WAS SCARCE on the busy farm, but much appreciated when it finally did come. The boys did find time to play with their neighbors on Sunday afternoons after returning from church, and they usually traveled to Columbus, Mississippi, the nearest big town, on Saturday afternoons.

"Papa believed in hard work and thought fishing and hunting were a waste of time. However, he did take us fishing one day each year. One of the requirements was that we had to catch live minnows for bait. Thurston and I enjoyed this. We were only about three-quarters of a mile from the branch and during lunch hour we would put out minnow baskets and run and get the minnows, and keep them in water until we got enough to go fishing.

"My daddy would put out set hooks on poles and stick them into the bank of Yellow Creek. The first time we went, we saw one of the poles on the other side of the creek bobbing up and down. My daddy pulled off his overalls, waded into the creek, and followed the line, reaching down and getting the fish by its gill. When he drew it up, he had an eight-pound trout. It was the most beautiful fish I had ever seen then, or since. The next year, we landed a ten-pound yellow catfish. It wasn't as pretty, but the eating was good," Faulkner grins.

Slipping off at lunch time was a tempting distraction for the Faulkner boys. They liked to go down to the backwater that stood alongside the railroad that passed through the pasture. Both parents had told them not to do it.

"It was the last time that I got a whipping, and my brother also got one. We decided to slip off and play in the stagnant water. We, of course, were late getting back and Mom had a switch for each of us and Pop had a switch for each of us. That ended our lunch time disobedience," he remembers.

"Living on a farm, we naturally loved to hunt and fish. Although our daddy thought it was a waste of time, we did get away some. Because we only lived about a mile from Yellow Creek, and the swamp started even closer to us, we would often go and hunt squirrels, which we would eat. One year, we set coon traps and caught two coons, which brought us $9.50. This was good money, and my brother used it to buy a double-barrel shotgun that had what was called an 'easy trigger.' One day, we were standing out on the porch and he put a shell into the chamber. I don't know just what happened, but when he went to shoot it, I guess he held it too high when the gun went off, because it shot a hole right through the ceiling. It scared him to death and Papa would have worn us both out if he found out about it. So Thurston got some white adhesive tape and sealed over the one-and-a-half-inch hole and, fortunately, father never saw it," Faulkner recalls.

Another gun mishap when Faulkner was nine years old still brings him nightmares.

"One day, Thurston was out on this log, checking a trap. I had this little .410 gauge shotgun that my uncle Dewey had given me. It was a dandy. Well, it went off and hit the log that Thurston was on. How it went off, I don't know, but fortunately it didn't hit him. And I don't think he ever knew how near he came to getting shot. I have thought a thousand times how lucky I was that he didn't."

HOLIDAYS WERE SPECIAL in the Faulkner household, and especially Christmas.

"Papa was frugal and would not let us buy but fifty-cents worth of firecrackers, which we enjoyed shooting during the holidays. Each Christmas we would hang our stocking on the mantel and we could always expect to have one orange, one apple, sometimes one banana, one box of sparklers and two or three pieces of penny candy in them. We would usually get a present from our parents, such as a shirt or pair of overalls, sometimes socks or shoes. Christmas was fun, and I was very disappointed when I learned at the age of about six or seven that Santa Claus was not for real."

The Faulkner boys didn't have to spend time deciding what to wear. It was always overalls and a blue denim shirt, worn around the barn, the house, and then to school. A few times in winter they would wear coveralls over the overalls and long johns to keep them warm in the biting cold winds.

"I wasn't too old when I discovered that wearing the same clothes to school that I wore to milk the cows was not a very popular thing with the people who stood or sat near me. Toward the end of the week, when it was about to become bath time on Saturday, the clothes began having a strong, unpleasant odor of soured milk. If Mom ever noticed it, she never mentioned it to me. But finally, as I got a little older, I did clean up a little more," Faulkner confessed.

"I was always very fond of reading and Papa always gave me a way to make a little money, like having a cotton patch or raising a pig, so that I could order from Sears and Roebuck a book that cost sixty-seven cents. Usually it was *Tom Swift*, or *The Bobsey Twins*, or we could actually buy Horatio Alger's books, like *Bound to Rise*, from Woolworth's 5 & 10 Cent Store for twenty cents. I read every book that I could get my hands on, which wasn't very many."

Summer was a special time for the entire community. About mid-July every year all the families would put aside their chores and head for the community of Sunny Side for the annual picnic. Sunny Side had a natural spring with plenty of cold, running water. Everyone from three to four miles around would come together and set up stands where cold drinks and lemonade were sold, and someone would be delegated to make the trip to nearby Columbus to fetch a five-gallon can of vanilla ice cream, which was sold in cones for a nickel.

One of the memories that stands out in Jimmy's childhood was the Sunny Side picnic that became known as "the Brunswick Stew Fight."

"Abe Russell, my uncle Dewey's wife's step-father, was noted for his temper. They were cooking Brunswick stew at the picnic and Mr. Russell was in charge. He insisted that no Irish potatoes be put in his stew. Well, the ladies didn't like that and they gave some potatoes to my cousin, Lloyd Varnon, who went and dumped them into the stew. This infuriated Mr. Russell, who got the stirring stick and hit Lloyd on the shoulder. At the same time, another cousin, Parnell Varnon, came riding up over a little rise on his mule and saw what was going on. He jumped off and sailed through the air and hit Mr. Russell and knocked him ten or fifteen feet. Mr. Russell then grabbed a .32 Colt pistol from his overalls pocket and drew it, but fortunately my father was there and knocked his arm up into the air, so no damage was done. Well, Mr. Russell went home and the rest of us went ahead with the picnic with the Brunswick stew, potatoes and all."

Abe Russell's temper never cooled. Once when Dewey's wife, Edna, was visiting her mother, Russell got into a fight with his wife (Edna's mother) and Edna tried to intervene. Russell got so upset he tried to choke Edna. She concealed the event from her husband as long as she could, but eventually told him. When Dewey found out about it, he slammed the door and headed out to kill Russell. Fortunately, Henry Faulkner was alerted and was able to stop his brother and reason with him enough to calm him down, at least for the moment.

"Later, they were having a revival one night at the Asbury Methodist Church. Dewey, Edna, and my grandmother were getting into the car. When the car light shined on Mr. Russell, Dewey saw him and got so mad he jumped on him. Parnell and Lloyd were also present, and they beat him pretty badly. No real damage was done and no arrests were made, and as far as I know this was the last of the incident, but everybody talked about it for years," Faulkner said.

My childhood home I see again,
And saddened with the view;
And still, as memory clouds my brain,
There's pleasure in it too.

Abraham Lincoln

2

Youth and Education

T he colorful and memorable childhood of young Jimmy came to a tragic halt when he was twelve years old. For eight years, the family had been living in their new home which Henry Faulkner had built near a free-flowing artesian well in the Star community not far from Vernon. On this cool October evening, Jimmy's older brother, Thurston, was away at the University of Alabama. It was bedtime, and Jimmy had already gone alone to the back bedroom for the evening. In the front bedroom, his parents were preparing to retire and his father reached to adjust the Coleman lamp.

Suddenly, the chilling screams of pain brought young Jimmy tearing through the house. He saw the flash of fire leaping from his parents' bedroom. His father was engulfed in flames and he yelled for his young son to get help as he ran from the house and headed for the trough of cool well water out back. The water brought only temporary relief and may have even made matters worse. Henry Faulkner died two days later, October 24, 1928, in the Columbus hospital. He was forty-five. On a clear fall day, at Shiloh Methodist

Church, Henry Faulkner was laid to rest next to his parents.

The horrible fire would play over and over in the mind of the young boy for years to come.

"I cried for days and days. We all loved him so much and depended on him. It was so hard for me. Finally, I cried so much our next-door neighbor, Cousin Lizzie Davis, tried to snap me out of it and said, 'Stop crying James, it could have been your mother!' I stopped crying then because there was nothing more precious in my life than my sweet mother, and I realized that I could have lost her.

"But it still becomes a nightmare for me anytime I smell burning gasoline. It all comes back to me because when I ran from the back bedroom to the front bedroom, it was all ablaze and, of course, I could smell gasoline because it was a gasoline fire.

"Incidentally, the last time I was in the old homeplace in 1984, I could still see scars from the fire in the front bedroom. How he got it put out, I don't know. I guess the gasoline just burnt up before it could catch anything on fire," Faulkner recalls.

After his father's death, young Jimmy struggled to overcome the experience.

"I always kept busy. I worked in my Uncle Ed's store. I thought that I was earning my keep but I found out much later that my Mom had actually paid him to hire me. And I remember at one time Mr. T. S. Jones, the president of the bank there, was the treasurer of a civic club and members would get behind in their pay, and he would get me to go around and collect for him. He would usually give me a dollar for doing this.

"But mainly, I just made myself love my mother that much more, and devoted my time and attention to her. It was really difficult for her but she realized that she just had to keep going. She was so lonesome, and I felt so sorry for her. I was very close to my mother and really, everything I did, I did it for her.

"My mother was one of fourteen children and she had some fine brothers and sisters, but not many of them achieved an education. One of her brothers became a doctor in Paul's Valley, Oklahoma, and another a lawyer in Bristow, Oklahoma. Uncle Andrew taught school, and as I recall, none of the others received a college education. The doctor, Uncle Luther, often said my mother was one of the finest business people of anyone that he knew.

"When Papa died, he did not leave us much, but in better condition than most. He actually had $1,000 in savings at Columbus National Bank. We sold the dairy cows for $500 and my mother made a little teaching school. My Uncle Ed owed Papa $1,000 that he had borrowed. I remember that when I was about eight or ten years old, we were working in one of the upper fields and Uncle Ed came to the farm and walked all the way up there to ask my dad to lend him the $1,000 to go into the mercantile business in Vernon. So after my father died, Uncle Ed gave my mother an old house next to where he lived for that debt, so my mom, my brother and I moved to Vernon and lived in that house. We were not wealthy, but neither were we considered poor. Fact is, we were quite fortunate in many respects."

It was a sad day for the family as they took one last look at the spacious home their dad had built for them, but they knew they could not stay there and live with the horrible memories of such a tragedy. Thurston was home from college during the holiday break. They sought to comfort each other, but they realized life would never be the same.

"Papa had bought the farm when he was about twenty-seven from Uncle Francis Varnon, who had married Dad's oldest sister, Aunt Birdie Faulkner Varnon. Papa had built a fine, new farm home and a new barn, and it was nothing like it was when he bought the place. But my mom felt that Aunt Birdie should have the house because she was a widow now, so she moved in with her three boys, a young daughter, and another daughter who was already married," Faulkner recalled.

As Jimmy's father had let the boys have a pig or a calf to raise, or a small cotton patch to farm, Jimmy had accumulated $300 in savings at the time his father died. Unfortunately, at the recommendation of his uncle, he loaned another uncle and his friend his entire savings so they could buy a sawmill. Although they gave the young boy a mortgage on the mill and agreed to pay 8 percent interest, Jimmy only collected one year's interest payment. Later he did receive half his money from one of the partners, but not the half from his uncle.

The smaller house in Vernon was an adjustment for the Faulkner family as Miss Ebbie looked after her growing boys and sought to complete her own college degree. The boys' Uncle Ed and Aunt Adine were kind and considerate, but that did not ease the loneliness of a family that had lost its father in such an untimely, unexpected tragedy.

Thurston had gone back to the University of Alabama in Tuscaloosa but in the summer, they all moved to Columbus, Mississippi, where Miss Ebbie enrolled in the Mississippi State College for Women. They stayed with another uncle and aunt, Anabel and Marvin Coleman, who operated a small family store. While his mother was in college, Jimmy worked in a department store for a dollar a day and also took a summer typing course, an achievement of great benefit to a young man who would later become a newspaper publisher and write columns for the rest of his life.

When summer ended, Miss Ebbie and Jimmy headed back to Vernon for the fall term of school. Thurston was expected to return to the University of Alabama but, to the dismay of his mother, he and a friend struck out instead to Silver City, New Mexico. Thurston soon began sending glowing reports to his mother and, over time, eventually persuaded her to pack up Jimmy and spend the summer in Silver City. Thurston had rented a place for the family to stay while Miss Ebbie attended a state teachers college and Jimmy delivered newspapers to help support the family.

When the family headed back to Vernon after the summer, they were already planning their return to New Mexico so Miss Ebbie could finish her college degree. The family stayed in Vernon for a year. In the spring, their mother took a year off and they packed up the little two-door '28 Chevrolet for the trip to Silver City. Jimmy was only thirteen, but he drove the entire trip because his mother could not drive. Five days and thirteen flat tires later, they arrived.

"Both Mother and I went to school. Thurston had just started teaching and had obligated himself to operating a little delicatessen-like store right in front of the college. We called it the 'Campus Cooler.' All three of us took turns working there when we were not in classes but we didn't make much, so later I had to work in a grocery store as well.

"They paid teachers more in New Mexico than they did in Alabama. Thurston made more as a beginning teacher than my mother had earned with many years of experience. In fact, my mother taught school for thirty-nine years and never made as much as a thousand dollars in any one year. The first school was a three-month school that paid her twenty-five dollars a month, and she had to pay five dollars of that for room and board," Faulkner recalled.

Jimmy was only fifteen when he entered his senior year of high school. During the year, he joined the National Guard and spent summer camp in Las Vegas, New Mexico. The young senior also played trombone in the school band, participated in Glee Club and played tennis. His lanky, lightweight frame proved too frail for football and he was soon sidelined with injuries.

Graduation day was a family affair; Jimmy and Miss Ebbie graduated the same year. While Jimmy clutched his high school diploma, his mother received her college degree from New Mexico State Teachers College; she had achieved her dream through years of chasing correspondence classes, summer schools, and extension courses. It was perhaps the brightest day for the family since they moved away from the old homeplace.

ON THE WAY HOME TO ALABAMA, the conversation centered on college. To Miss Ebbie, it was an ineluctable conclusion that her son would attend a Christian school.

Jimmy's cousin and two friends back in Vernon had already decided to attend Freed-Hardeman, a church of Christ junior college in Henderson, Tennessee. It didn't take his friends long to convince Jimmy that this was where he should spend his college days. Miss Ebbie knew that the school had an excellent reputation and was known for producing preachers and Bible scholars.

When it was time to pack for college, Jimmy didn't own a suit, so his mother took him to Columbus, Mississippi, to find one.

"I tried on one that cost seventeen dollars, but they had another one that was twenty-two dollars, and looked much better. Finally, after much consideration, my mother decided she wanted me to have the best, so we paid twenty-two dollars for the blue suit. I had a suit, an extra pair of pants and three or four shirts, and that was it. Fortunately, my roommate, Ray B. Hankins, and I were the same size. He also had one suit, so we would switch, and that gave us a change that we thought was very nice.

"I was standing behind Ray in this long line of students who were waiting to register. I could hear them being asked about what they wanted to study. I hadn't really thought much about it because I was just overwhelmed at being at the school, I guess. Finally, I asked Ray what he was going to study, and he said, 'journalism.'

"I said, 'Ray, what does that mean?'

"And he told me that it was writing and working for newspapers. So when it came my time at the head of the line, I told them that I wanted to study journalism. At the time, of course, I never dreamed that I would own a chain of newspapers."

It didn't take the enterprising journalism student long to get started. He convinced the school's president, N. B. Hardeman, that the institution should have a public relations person, and since Faulkner was a journalism student, who better could fit the position? The young student landed the job, earning one hundred dollars a year to help pay his college expenses. And with this experience and title, he was able to get jobs as a "stringer" for several area newspapers covering college sports, adding a few more dollars to help pay the way.

Faulkner continued to play the trombone through junior college, but gave up the instrument after that. He did sing in the glee club, but never considered himself a very good singer. In general, social life was quite limited on the Christian college campus.

"The only time we were allowed to date at Freed-Hardeman was on Sunday night. We marched about a block from the girl's dormitory and went to church. Then we marched straight back to the dormitories and everybody would stay in the living room of the dormitory and promptly at 10, the boys had to go home. The president of the college frowned on boys and girls getting too friendly back then. Now, of course, that has changed.

"Although I had many dates, it was usually with a different girl every Sunday night. I was sort of bashful growing up, but I did gather more photographs of girls than any other boy on the campus," Faulkner boasts.

JIMMY FAULKNER WAS barely a teenager when the stock market crashed in October 1929, plunging the nation into the Great Depression. Unemployment increased, many farmers lost their land, families lost their homes, and thousands of banks closed with customers losing their life's savings. It was a trying time for a widowed mother to raise her family and send two boys to college.

"It was not a very good experience," Faulkner recalls. "But as I look back over it, it probably was a fine thing for me because it taught me that there are a lot of things you don't have to have. We always had a little food and very few clothes, but no luxury. We thought we were doing well because many people didn't have any more, and most had less," he added.

"Politicians ran on a platform of 'a chicken in every pot.' That sounds ridiculous today, but back then a chicken was a luxury. There weren't enough to go around for hungry people. I remember my uncle Clarence Greer would buy cheap shotgun shells, kill rabbits, take them to Columbus, Mississippi, and sell them for ten cents apiece. Then, he would take the money and buy more shells to kill more rabbits. And rabbits were not plentiful, either," Faulkner stressed.

In 1932, incumbent president Herbert Hoover faced stiff opposition from Franklin D. Roosevelt, who offered the American people a "New Deal" of innovative measures to counteract the effects of the Great Depression.

"My mother was for Hoover because she was a Republican. I was driving her to Trull Beat, about fifteen miles south of Vernon, to vote for Hoover when I rounded a curve and another car was coming from the opposite direction. There was not enough room for us to pass, so we ran off the road. My mother never got to vote. Hundreds of times after that, in making speeches, I would joke and say that this taught me to never vote Republican, and I never did for many years," Faulkner remembers.

Roosevelt's overwhelming victory in 1932 opened the way for a flood of new federal programs to jump-start the economy and restore faith in the nation's future.

"Roosevelt was a great speaker and a great savior of the country, considering the depth of the depression which left so many people hungry. He was always very popular with the people, especially when he would get on the radio and speak."

Faulkner himself was a beneficiary of one of the first federal programs. At the end of his freshman year at Freed-Hardeman, at the age of seventeen, he landed a good-paying summer job.

"I got a job with AAA (Agriculture Adjustment Agency), figuring acreage on a Monroe calculator so people could plow up cotton. I made twelve dollars a week, and very happy to do so since I was living at home with my mother. The idea was to help farmers who couldn't sell cotton. The government would get farmers to plow up cotton fields and pay them for it. We had people who would go out and measure the fields, and I would calculate the acreage. It was an excellent job."

And just how was a teenager able to land a high-paying job like that?

"It was political," he laughs.

"The county agent was dating a lady who was staying with my mother. The young woman was a home economics teacher from Brilliant, a Miss Grenade, and she was teaching in Vernon. The County Agent, T. A. Carnes, visited my mother's home a lot to see Miss Grenade, and that's where I got to meet him. And of course, I had the added advantage that I knew how to use the calculator.

"I could have gotten the job of going out into the field and measuring, and that paid fifteen dollars a week, but that previous spring I had an appendicitis operation in Jackson, Tennessee, near Freed-Hardeman. Back then, if you had any type of operation they figured you were not able to do physical hard work for months.

"I worked in the office with a young lady who did the same thing I did. She was Martha Stone Cobb, a beautiful girl and a lovely person who really needed the job. Later she became the wife of Birmingham industrialist Hugh Daniels," Faulkner said.

The extra money provided a needed boost as Faulkner returned to Freed-Hardeman to conclude his second year.

Faulkner had heard that the best journalism school in the nation was the University of Missouri. By working hard, using what little money he had saved, and with the continued help of his mother, he was determined to give it his best.

When he enrolled at the University of Missouri, he discovered that his Southern accent actually complemented his popularity.

"The accent was not that distinctive because there were quite a few others there from the South. I didn't mind it at all. What bothered me was when I went back home, people made fun of me because they said I had lost my Southern brogue, and I guess maybe I had. For a Southerner to go off and come back home not knowing how to talk was bad," Faulkner laughs.

"But I guess I overcame that problem because when I go up North now, people can tell I'm from the South," he says.

Attending the University of Missouri was a huge step, both financially and academically.

"Upon arriving at the school, I did not know where I was going to stay. Several fraternities were rushing me, and I spent miserable hours trying to get away from them because I did not have the money to join a fraternity. But my senior year, I borrowed a little money and joined Kappa Alpha, largely because it was a Southern organization and because they seemed to be anxious to have me. I never lived in the house, but I did eat night meals there, which was about the only regular meals I had during school.

"I felt it was important to join a good fraternity on campus," he adds.

As usual, Faulkner's mother approved of what he did, and did not object to his joining Kappa Alpha.

Located not far from the campus in Columbia were two all-girl schools, Stevens College for Women and Columbia Christian College.

"The Christian college was about three miles off, but they had the most beautiful girls, many of them from Kentucky. Many times I would walk over there and walk back with them to town, never having enough money to get a taxi. This was not the popular thing to do with some girls.

"Only once or twice did I go to Stevens, but I did date some of the University's girls. I was younger than most of them and felt somewhat ill at ease because of this. In fact, I don't think I ever dated a girl at the university that wasn't a year or two older, which seemed important to me at the time."

EVEN BEFORE HIS graduation in 1936, Faulkner returned to his home in Vernon where he began to look for employment. He first approached the editor and publisher of the Columbus, Mississippi, *Commercial Dispatch*, Birney Imes, who quickly told him no. Imes, in positive terms, told him there was no future for a journalism graduate. He maintained it was a complete waste of time to go to a journalism school.

"Mr. Imes told me that he was sending his own son, Birney

Imes, Jr., to Ole Miss, not to learn anything about newspapers, but for a social life and to learn about the people of Mississippi. He told me that he had been approached to run for Lieutenant Governor of Mississippi, and that he had started in the newspaper business by sweeping floors and working his way up to become editor and publisher.

"I told him that I had no floors to sweep, since I was born on a farm, and then I left somewhat disappointed," Faulkner recalls, explaining that the idea in those days among many old-time publishers was that journalism school was a nuisance and a waste of time.

Interestingly, two or three years later Birney would write a fine editorial about Faulkner's progress as publisher of a newspaper in Alabama.

Faulkner returned to campus to complete his studies, but with no prospect of a job after graduation.

It was a beautiful, clear day and the graduation ceremony at the University of Missouri was held outside. Although Faulkner's mother could not make the trip—neither time nor money was available—he marched proudly in the procession and tightly clenched his diploma. The young graduate was deeply warmed by a feeling of accomplishment. He had worked at two jobs to pay his way through college, along with the help he had received from his mother, and both were proud that he had finished owing only five hundred dollars.

"At the time, if I could have found a job that paid two hundred dollars a month, I would have signed up for life," Faulkner remembers.

Persistence

Nothing in the world can take the place of persistence. Talent will not — nothing is more common than unsuccessful men with talent. Genius will not — unrewarded genius is almost a proverb. Education alone will not — the world is full of educated derelicts. Persistence, Determination and Hard Work make the difference.

Plaque on wall of Jimmy Faulkner's office

Son, work hard, be honest, go to church, and when
you get to a high fence that looks impossible to climb,
God will take you by the nape of the neck and the seat
of the pants and lift you over it.

Ebbie Faulkner

3

A Career Begins

I n the shadow of the passing Great Depression, a Bachelor of Journalism degree did not guarantee immediate employment with a newspaper, or anywhere else, for a twenty-year-old graduate. Being unsuccessful in finding a job in nearby Columbus, Mississippi, Faulkner's next attempt took him to Montgomery. Armed with a letter of recommendation from a family friend, he hitched a ride to Alabama's capital city to meet with Cash Stanley, editor of the *Alabama Journal*. Stanley did not need anyone.

Faulkner filled in for a week at his local newspaper, the *Lamar Democrat* in Vernon, while the owner, Lee Barnes, took a vacation. Barnes complimented the young newspaperman's editorial skills, and wanted to sell him half interest in the *Democrat* if he could come up with the money. Faulkner decided he had rather own a newspaper than to work for one. He and his mother, who stood by him in his risky decision, visited the local bank and were told by the president that the bank did not consider such a loan a wise investment. Although greatly disappointed, Faulkner would later be thankful for the rejection. The small town held very limited opportunity for a young man with great dreams.

A visit to another newspaper, the *Northwest Alabamian* in Fayette, steered the youthful newspaperman in a life-changing direction. Faulkner had been told that the paper's owner was willing to sell, but at the last minute the man changed his mind. Instead, he told Faulkner about a publication called the *Baldwin Times* in a small south Alabama town called Bay Minette, and that owner R. V. (Bob) Vail was willing to sell.

That Vail was willing to sell was only half true. He would sell just half ownership at first, and consider the other half later.

"On August 15, 1936, I bought half of the *Baldwin Times* for $3,750, paying $1,500 down payment.

"Of course, my mother knew absolutely nothing about the newspaper, and neither did I. We discussed the financial possibilities and responsibilities about buying the *Baldwin Times*. She was deliberate and cautious, because as a schoolteacher she never made as much as $1,000 in a year and she had to be frugal. But she did have confidence in me, that I would work hard and, if possible, make it. For this reason, she was willing to mortgage her only possession, her home, for the $1,500 down payment. Some of her relatives told her she was foolish, that I would never make it, but she did so anyway to get me started in the newspaper business.

"Six months later, Mr. Vail decided to sell me the other half of the paper. After we had settled, I asked him the question, 'Mr. Vail, why wouldn't you sell me all of it to start with?'

"He said, 'Three reasons. First, I wanted to make sure you could do a better job for the people of this area than I did. Secondly, I wanted to make sure you were a Democrat. And thirdly, I wanted to be sure that you would be a friend of Lister Hill.'

"That's the way he put it. Senator Hill at that time was a congressman in this district and had gotten Vail appointed postmaster, so he was loyal to him. Actually, all three of those conditions were easy because I was a Democrat and a friend of Hill. It certainly was no difficulty doing a better job than he did, not that he didn't have the ability, he just lacked the interest. He had a big family and couldn't feed them with the paper, frankly. He also had the Rex Theater that his wife ran.

"So before I was twenty-one years old, I owed over twelve thousand dollars, and in 1936 that was a huge amount of money."

It would take about five years to repay the mortgage on his mother's home, but Faulkner would remain in debt for more than half a century.

"Some ten years after I paid the mortgage, I would tell people that I was an optimist and expected to get out of debt someday. And I still do," Faulkner laughs.

What was it like the first time he walked into his *Baldwin Times* office?

"I walked in, and there were two people in there. One was Mr. Vail's daughter, Mary, who was going over the subscription list, which was probably less than three hundred. Her daddy had told her that every subscription that she sold or collected, she could have.

"Then, the printer, Cotton Taylor, was there. He was Vail's only employee, and he made twelve dollars a week.

"There was no ceiling, no office, really, just a corner of the room where the roll-top desk was located. There was a Model Five Underwood typewriter, no adding machine, no cash box or anything. There was no running water and no heat. Of course, it was August when I came and we didn't need any heat. There were no fans, no decent lights. It was a fifteen-hundred square-foot building that was built at a cost of $750. It was really desolate."

FAULKNER'S NEW BUSINESS quarters included a rustic staircase that

took up much-needed space in the all-purpose office room. It led
to the roof of the little building where the previous owner had
fashioned a small, wood-framed structure intended to be his private office. However, these plans never developed because about
that time Vail became postmaster and lost interest in the *Baldwin
Times.*

"The little office was no more than twelve by fifteen feet, and I
used to go up there and try to make engraving plates so that I would
be able to print pictures. I spent many nights up there trying, but
was never successful.

"But I discovered a little safe up there; I guess it was about two
feet by three feet. When I mentioned it to Mr. Vail, he told me that
he could not get it open, and said, 'Just keep that.'

"Later, I was able to hire a second person, a Linotype operator,
at fifteen dollars a week. He was also an electrician, and a wizard. He
could set type, do anything, even open safes. So one night, when
everything was quiet, he went up there and listened to the safe's
tumblers, and opened it. In the safe was a roster of the local Ku Klux
Klan, and Mr. Vail had been the secretary. They didn't call it
secretary because they had a certain name for it.

"Well, I looked at the list, just glanced at it, and every prominent person in Bay Minette was a member. Well, I knew he didn't
want that published, so I just took it over to him at the post office.
He grabbed it, and he was glad to get it. He thanked me for bringing
it to him. I'm sure he must have burned it.

"I should have kept that list, because it would have made an
interesting story at some time. The probate judge, the circuit clerk,
the mayor . . . all were members of the Ku Klux Klan. I should have
kept it, but I didn't.

"There must have been sixty or seventy names on that list. Of
course, I did not want to embarrass anybody, but I could have

written an article for the *Saturday Evening Post* and made more money than I was making publishing the *Baldwin Times*, but I would have had to move out of town," Faulkner smiles.

Did Faulkner have any idea Vail was a member of the Ku Klux Klan at the time be bought the newspaper?

"Oh no. He probably wrote editorials against the Ku Klux Klan. I don't remember that, but he probably did. But that was in 1936. Hugo Black was appointed by Roosevelt to the United States Supreme Court in 1937. Later, a writer for the *Philadelphia Enquirer* wrote a series of articles on Black. In his research, he discovered that Black was a member of the Ku Klux Klan. That reporter got a Pulitzer prize for that. He could have asked anybody in Alabama, and they would have told him that Black would not have been elected Senator had he not been a member of the Ku Klux Klan."

Black, a native of Clay County, Alabama, attended the University of Alabama, served as a prosecuting attorney in Jefferson County, and was elected to the U. S. Senate in 1926. After his appointment as associate justice of the United States Supreme Court, Black supported racial desegregation in public life.

Finally, Faulkner tore down the little structure on the roof of the building because he needed the office space that was taken up by the stairs.

For this cause shall a man leave father and mother, and shall cleave to his wife.

Matthew 19:5

4

A Porch Swing Romance

Taking over a newspaper proved a financial struggle for Faulkner. The first year of operation grossed six thousand dollars, out of which came mortgage payments, loan payments for a new Linotype, with just a few dollars left over for food and rent.

When Faulkner arrived in Bay Minette, he boarded with Mrs. G. L. Lambert, a doctor's widow who lived within a block of where he worked.

"There was no heat in the bathroom and I continuously had a cold, but the food was good, for a ditch digger," he remembers.

But the prospect of a brighter business future was not the only thing that sparked the young publisher's attention. On the way to work, each day he would stroll by the white-framed home on the corner where Mrs. Ella Irwin lived with her petite young daughter, Evelyn.

"The first time I saw Evelyn was when I was walking by their house. I guess I stopped and talked to her and her mother. I remember that they had a swing, and in the summer, we would sit outside in the swing. In the winter, I would sit inside with them and talk."

"She was the first person I ever dated in Bay Minette. In fact, she was the only one. I was with other girls in crowds, but never on a date. She and her mother had a car, and I didn't have one. Sometimes we would ride around in the car, but there was really nowhere to go on dates.

"Evelyn had a good job at the courthouse, which was right across the street from the *Times*, so I would visit her there from time to time. She also was the organist for the Methodist church and the pastor lived right across the street from where I lived. I guess we all got to know each other pretty fast."

In less than a year after they met, Jimmy and Evelyn borrowed her mother's two-door Ford and drove to Evergreen, in Conecuh County, where they were married April 15, 1937.

"There wasn't a ceremony. We just went into the probate judge's office. I called Mr. Gaston, the editor and publisher of the paper, who was a friend of mine, and he was our best man. We were married there in the office, then we drove on up to Montgomery and spent our honeymoon in the Whitley Hotel. From Montgomery, we went on up to Vernon to visit Mom and give her the news," Faulkner recalled.

The young couple moved into a furnished apartment on Railroad Street; they paid twelve dollars a month rent. On May 31, 1938, Jimmy and Evelyn welcomed their first son into the world, James Herman Faulkner, Jr.

It would be awhile before the family decided it could afford a home of their own. Finally, they found just what they wanted, a little two-bedroom home on East Fifth Street. It cost $2,200, but there was no down payment and the monthly payment was only $14.40. This would be the Faulkner home for the next eighteen years.

It was in the front bedroom of this home that their youngest son, Wade, was born on January 29, 1941. Dr. J. C. McLeod said that Evelyn did not need to go to the hospital. The entire cost, including pre- and post-natal care, was twenty-five dollars, the same amount McLeod charged when Jimmy, Jr., was born. The same doctor who delivered both children also had delivered their mother.

Son, work hard, be honest, go to church, and when you get to a high fence that looks impossible to climb, God will take you by the nape of the neck and the seat of the pants and lift you over it

Ebbie Faulkner

5

A Dark Cloud Gathers

T he sun was finally rising and shining brightly on Faulkner's career. The young publisher had the newspaper under control, he had made his mark on the small town, and there was even a movement under way to elect this recent newcomer mayor. At twenty-four, he was destined to be dubbed, "The youngest mayor in America," a distinction no one really ever tried to document. News of the electoral victory delighted Faulkner's mother.

But just as things seemed their brightest, a black cloud loomed. Ebbie Faulkner became ill. When her condition deteriorated, she was taken to the nearby hospital in Fayette.

"She had never used a doctor except when Thurston and I were born. She didn't take medicine, she just didn't go to a doctor. She never needed one until this happened," Faulkner recalls.

The doctor sadly announced that Ebbie Faulkner had a condition known as a streptococcal infection of the heart. There was no effective treatment for "strep heart" at that time because there was no way to get the medication to the heart. The virus would later be treated effectively with penicillin.

"Four years later they had the medicine that would have cured her, but they didn't have it then. I would drive up there every weekend and stay overnight. Frankly, I would cry on the way up there and cry on the way back. I would take little Jimmy with me. He was just a toddler at the time, but she always wanted to see him.

"My brother was living in Fayette at the time and was a vocational agriculture teacher there. He helped care for her while she was sick," Faulkner adds.

Jimmy and Thurston were with her when she passed away.

Faulkner was only twelve when his father died in the tragic fire; now, twelve years later, he had lost the person who had the most influence on his life.

"I don't think she had great expectations of us, as far as being successful in business. She did have great expectations of us as far as morality and things of that nature.

"She told me, 'Son, work hard, be honest, go to church, and when you get to a high fence that looks impossible to climb, God will take you by the nape of the neck and the seat of the pants and lift you over it,'" Faulkner remembers.

It was the biggest funeral ever held in Vernon. All the area schools closed so that teachers, students, and former students could pay tribute to the dear friend they called, "Miss Ebbie," "Aunt Ebbie," or "Cousin Ebbie."

"At the time she died, she was a mathematics teacher at Lamar County High School. Students and former students lined up several blocks from her home to the church," Faulkner said.

Ebbie Johnson Faulkner was only fifty-nine when she died on April 3, 1941. She was laid to rest beside her husband in the Shiloh cemetery near Pleasant Hill, where she once served as the principal of a three-teacher school early in her career.

"She was a great lady, a great woman. I was very close to my mother and really, everything I did, I did it for her. I wanted to please her. But when she died in 1941, everything I did after that, I did it to please my family."

Be not forgetful to entertain strangers; for thereby some have entertained angels unawares.

Hebrews 13:2

6

"Angels Unawares"

I t was daybreak on a Thursday morning in late August of 1938 and the sunlight was just beginning to pierce the cobwebbed windowpane on the front of the *Baldwin Times* office on courthouse square in Bay Minette. Jimmy Faulkner had worked all night, racing the clock to piece together another weekly edition of his newspaper. It was not the first time he had worked all Wednesday night to "put to bed" his publication. But this night he wrestled not only columns of type but also the looming question of where he would get the $1,500 payment due on his newspaper at the end of the year? He could see that he was going to be about a thousand dollars short.

But as he leaned back in his chair to enjoy the momentary pride of accomplishment in knowing that this week's paper was ready for the mail, he glanced up to see a battered Plymouth creak to a stop out front. A rumpled, warmly dressed man slid from beneath the steering wheel and soon appeared in the open doorway. The wiry, dark-haired man, standing no more than five-feet-eight, was sanguine and straight-forward.

"Morning," he said, extending a callused hand obviously accustomed to hard labor. "Hunnicutt's my name. Chester Hunnicutt."

After brief introductions, Faulkner learned that the town's newest stranger was an itinerant revival preacher desiring to place an ad to publicize his services. The visitor was in his mid-thirties but hard work and years of travel had weathered him beyond his years.

"I'm going home to eat breakfast and I'd be glad if you'd join me," Faulkner said. Inviting guests to his home to eat was a practice of the newspaper publisher throughout his life. Governors, United States senators, congressmen, mayors, foreign dignitaries, and yes, even preachers would follow the trail to the Faulkner home for the next sixty years, but it all started with this stranger.

Of course the ad did run in the newspaper, the preacher held his revival for several days, and then he left town. A few days later Faulkner received a letter postmarked Union, South Carolina. The preacher recounted the visit, saying that during his stay in town he had talked to a number of people and had found that Faulkner was doing a good job, and "a good work," and it had occurred to him that he might need some financial help.

Faulkner sat down and hand-wrote an answer, thanking Hunnicutt, and affirming that yes, he was concerned about a payment that was coming due at the end of the year, but felt he could make it some way. From the looks of the preacher's battered old car and his personal appearance, Faulkner assumed the man was thinking in terms of ten or perhaps even twenty dollars.

"Just a few days after I wrote him, as soon as the mail could deliver a return letter, he sent me a check for one thousand dollars, exactly the amount I needed. I went home, drew up a note for one thousand dollars, and my wife and I signed it and mailed it to him. He had sent me the check without any assurance that the money would ever be repaid," Faulkner said. "I tell you, it was a life saver. The upcoming payment was fifteen hundred dollars and I had only one-third of it. Still today, I don't know how I could have come up with the other thousand dollars without his help."

Ten years later, after Faulkner had become more involved with politics, he and his wife Evelyn, along with George Wallace and Roy Noland, Jr., attended the Democratic National Convention in Philadelphia. It was the year that Harry Truman was nominated. (Interestingly, Faulkner and Wallace stuck with the national party and refused to join the "Dixiecrat" revolt that emerged that year, largely over the issue of Truman's support for desegregation of the military and a civil rights bill.)

As they drove north, their route took them through the Carolinas.

"As we struck South Carolina, I said, 'I don't know where Union is, but wherever it is, we're going by there.'

"They asked me why I wanted to go to Union, and I told them the story of Chester Hunnicutt. George said, 'I don't blame you, we'll go.' And from that developed a great friendship with Mr. Hunnicutt," Faulkner said.

Faulkner describes the man as deeply honest, very frugal, and an interesting person. Hunnicutt and his wife, Thelma, were part Cherokee Indian and both were hard workers. Mrs. Hunnicutt had quit her job in an underwear factory in Tennessee where she made twenty-five cents an hour, and the two were married in 1937. During the early years of preaching, they lived on twenty-five dollars a week, but tithed every nickel.

"In the later years of his ministry, he made seventy-five dollars a week and dedicated seventeen dollars of that to the church, and gave even more to other church needs. But nearly everything he touched made good investments," Faulkner said.

"He was really the one who taught me to give. He said, 'Jimmy, you can't outgive God, but try.'"

Hunnicutt and his wife moved from Union, South Carolina, to Cherokee, North Carolina, to preach at a small church and to do mission work on the Indian reservation. One summer, he asked Faulkner to join evangelist V. P. Black in conducting a revival there.

"Evelyn and I stayed a week and I led singing for the Indians. I discovered that when you lead singing to Indians, you sing solo. Fortunately I had Evelyn, Brother Black and his wife, Brother Hunnicutt and his wife to help me. But the Indians sat there glum. It was quite an experience," Faulkner noted.

The thousand-dollar loan was only the first. When Faulkner was in military service, Hunnicutt loaned him another thousand. When the war was over, the preacher said, "Jimmy, anytime I get money, I sure would like to lend it to you, as long as you pay me the interest, because I trust you more than I do the banks."

Later, Faulkner and Hunnicutt went together and built a hotel in Cherokee, North Carolina, near the preacher's church building. Faulkner owned one-third of the motel. Hunnicutt and his wife worked there day and night. Finally, Faulkner gave them the investment he had put into the facility.

Hunnicutt also bought some land in Florida and, although he never became wealthy, he did quite well for a country preacher. He had abandoned the old Plymouth and drove a nice automobile.

Chester A. Hunnicutt died in 1979; he had requested that Faulkner conduct his funeral.

"It was the only funeral I have ever preached. The service was held in Dixon, Tennessee, and my brother, Thurston, rode up there with me. I remember the scripture I used about Barnabas:

For he was a good man, and full of the Holy Ghost and
of faith: and much people was added unto the Lord.

Acts 11:24

"I said that Chester Hunnicutt was like Barnabas; he was a good
man."

At the time of Hunnicutt's death Faulkner owed the preacher
$250,000 but his widow refused to accept payment for the debt at
that time, or anytime since. In fact, she has asked Faulkner to be
administrator of her affairs when she dies.

Since he wasn't allowed to repay the money directly, Faulkner
invested the $250,000 in bonds with written instructions how to
handle the obligation regarding her estate. Thelma Hunnicutt has
the financial security and the steadfast friendship she needs in her
sunset years.

"This lady doesn't realize how much help they were to me. And
yet, she tells me how lucky she has been to have known me, and how
fortunate it would be if every person in her condition had a friend
like me. And actually, during all those years I needed that money
very badly, and probably made a lot of money out of it. She lives in
Florence, Alabama, and I went to see her a few months ago. I still
call her at least once a month to see how she is doing."

At eighty-seven, Thelma Hunnicutt remains mentally sharp,
although not as physically active as she would like. She still drives to
church in her 1996 white Oldsmobile and, with the help of a cane,
walks the sidewalks near her apartment complex. Although she
endures a daily struggle with diabetes and other physical distractions, she remains independent and has a sharp mind and keen
sense of humor. On the twentieth anniversary of the death of her
husband, she sat in her upholstered platform rocker and reflected:

"I had the best husband in the world. We married in 1937. I had dated a boy for several years that I went to school with, and Chester came along. We had six dates and got married. He had started preaching after he graduated from Burritt Bible College up on the mountain in Tennessee, and was in our area for a meeting. That's how I met him. They didn't pay preachers much then, and Chester would never ask for money. We worked at different things, and I made all my clothes, even my coats, and sewed for other people and worked in stores. But we took care of ourselves," she said.

"We moved a lot and lived in six different states. It got to where I was like the farmer's chickens. The farmer had moved so many times that every time the chickens heard him walking down the path, they would lie down and cross their legs so they could be tied and thrown into the wagon. That's how they moved chickens back then," she laughed, "tied their legs so they couldn't jump out."

Pointing to the picture of an attractive, young brunette on her den wall, she said, "That's Chester's first wife there," waiting stone-faced for a reaction.

"It's also his only wife," she chuckles, explaining the portrait of herself that was made when she was in her thirties.

"Nearly every time we moved back then, we would rent a place for awhile and then build a house. Chester was not a carpenter, but my father was, and I knew a lot about it and taught my husband. We built at least six houses. I even drew up the plans and helped build. I was hauling shingles to the roof on a ladder when I was carrying my first baby. One day I told Chester, this is the last load I'm bringing up. From now on you can bring your own. A couple of school boys working with him didn't know what I meant, but Chester knew," she said.

She misses her own home, but concedes that being in her modest apartment near the oldest of her two sons is best for her. Stroking back her short-cropped silver hair, she admits her loneliness.

"I came down here to be close to my kids but they stay gone a lot. Being eighty-seven years old, I've had a lot of experiences and I have enjoyed life. It's a lonely life now, and I've always been a person who enjoyed people; I just grew up that way. Really, you would not believe that people just don't come to visit you. When I was young, we were always close to our neighbors and my mother would go and wash clothes on a rub-board when a woman was in bed. I don't reckon I know anybody around here who would wash a handkerchief for me. But I get along, and I like it here."

A real highlight of her life is receiving the reliable telephone call from her friend, Jimmy Faulkner.

"Jimmy is the best friend I have in the world, I can tell you that. And I have heard him tell people a lot of times, 'Thelma is the only sister I ever had.' That's the way he feels about me. I've known him since he was real young. I don't know what I would do if anything happened to Jimmy. He calls me just like he was my brother. I'm a little older than Jimmy, but I love him like a brother. He is one in a million.

"I've got his picture sitting over there on the table," she says as she points proudly to a round table in the corner with a lamp and an eight-by-ten, black-and-white portrait. It is one that she and her husband received when Faulkner was running for governor many years ago.

"He's my guardian angel, I guess," she glows.

Ask Jimmy Faulkner the secret of his success and he'll tell you that whatever success he's achieved has been due to good luck. Probe him further and he'll admit that the harder you work, the more luck you have. He'll also tell you that one has to have sense enough to recognize opportunities and take advantage of them.

But was Hunnicutt's visit to the newspaper office in 1938 luck?

"In the first place, what was he doing in Bay Minette? In the second place, why did he drop by the place at the time that I needed help? And in the third place, why did he have any money, and was willing to trust me with it?

"So was it luck, providence, or a guardian angel? Maybe all three combined," Faulkner says smilingly.

> For he shall give his angels charge over thee,
> to keep thee in thy ways.
>
> Psalm 91:11

~

> But lay up yourselves treasures in heaven,
> where neither moth nor rust doth corrupt,
> and where thieves do not break through to steal:
> For where your treasure is,
> there will your heart be also.
>
> Matthew 6:20-21

7

Treasures of the Heart

High on the list of his early childhood memories are the "brush arbor" camp meetings and tent revivals Faulkner was forced to attend as a child. Such meetings were common in the twenties and thirties and were usually held out in the country at a time when farmers had completed the busy season of hard work. Church members would place poles upright into the ground, then other poles would be connected across the tops from one to another, so that brushes or pine twigs could be laid over them to form a make-shift roof. In some cases, tents would be used.

From the time Jimmy was about seven years old, Ebbie Faulkner tugged her reluctant young son to the "preaching meetings" held in their community.

"Brush arbors were no good against the rain, but they did keep the sun out. Most of the meetings were in the daytime, but I attended some night meetings when lanterns and coal oil lamps were used. I even remember on one occasion, sawdust was hauled in and scattered on the ground for a floor, but that was not true in most cases," Faulkner recalls.

"Brother Gus Nichols usually conducted the services, and he

was one of the most intelligent Bible scholars it has ever been my privilege to know. But he was one of the most long-winded, too, often speaking for two hours, and I was bored and probably did not listen.

"I did not look forward to these meetings, but I went because my mother told me to go. Often I would catch myself looking around for stray girls who could be talked into slipping out of the brush arbor and I would talk to them, or to other friends. I was not very good at listening to the preacher and probably did not receive much from the sermons," Faulkner remembers.

Despite the frequent distractions of both Jimmy and Thurston, Ebbie Faulkner continued to bring up her boys in the church and saw to their faithful attendance at all services.

"My mother was a member of the church of Christ and my father was a Methodist. He was not as devoted as my mother but read at least one chapter in the Bible every day. He was a good man. My mother was never able to convert him, but probably would have had he lived," Faulkner said.

The churches of Christ is a group of churches that have no overall organization or general assembly. Congregations are found in all fifty states and most countries of the world, but have long been more numerous in the South. In Alabama they are particularly strong in the Tennessee Valley and in south Alabama.

When Faulkner arrived in Baldwin County in 1936, there were only two congregations in the entire county with a total membership of less than one hundred. Now, there are thirteen congregations with combined membership of as many as three thousand. There are about one hundred forty members where Faulkner attends.

The churches of Christ were "restored" in the 1800s when Alexander Campbell and Barton W. Stone joined forces. They set out to restore the New Testament church, established around A.D. 33 in Jerusalem as recorded in the book of Acts, Chapter 2.

Campbell and Stone pleaded to reestablish the worship, ideals and plan of salvation as set out under the New Testament church. Members consider themselves as part of the original Christian church, not members of a present-day denomination. Their theme is to "speak where the Bible speaks and be silent where the Bible is silent."

In 1906, the U.S. census first officially recorded them as a separate religious body. Today, the churches of Christ continue to hold to the principles and practices of the New Testament church. They do not answer to headquarters of men placed in powerful positions — "only to God and his Holy Word" (Romans 2:2).

Individual congregations are autonomous and managed by members selected from the congregation, called elders, who are chosen according to the guidelines in Second Timothy and Titus. They look strictly to the New Testament for religious tenets. The worship service consists of reading and teaching from the Bible, prayer, the weekly observance of The Lord's Supper, contributions for church support, and the singing of hymns without instrumental accompaniment. To become a member, a person must believe in Jesus Christ as the Son of God, repent of one's sin, and be baptized by immersion for the remission of sins.

"My mother never pushed me about being baptized, but her teachings did eventually bear results. As a sixteen-year-old college freshman at Freed-Hardeman, I was baptized, largely by the influence of what I had learned growing up and by the influence of one of the greatest speakers I have ever heard, N. B. Hardeman. He was one of the greatest preachers of his era, and one of the most intelligent men I have ever known," Faulkner remembers.

The early influence of his mother had a lasting effect on

Faulkner's life and habits. "My mother taught me to be courteous and to address my elders by 'yes ma'am,' 'no ma'am,' 'yes sir,' and 'no sir,' 'mister' and 'misses.' She taught me that humbleness is very inexpensive, yet very profitable. I have tried to practice this throughout my life.

"My mother also taught me not to curse. When I was about five or six years old, I used curse words in front of her, and she told me not to do it. Then, I ran down the hall of our farm house yelling out, 'G— d— s.o.b.!' Again, she gently got me and took me into the front bedroom, sat me down on the bed, and talked to me ten or fifteen minutes, invoking God and other things, shaming me, which she had a great ability to do, for using ugly language. She stopped me forever. I haven't cursed since that time."

When he moved to Bay Minette to begin life on his own, one of the first things he looked for was the church of Christ. One of the first things he found was another tent, reminiscent of his youthful revival days.

"There were no more than about fifteen members, and I remember there was a little tent revival going on, and so, I started going. As it turned out, there were only two men in the congregation at the time who were regular attendees, myself and an elderly man, Mr. Wilson. Mr. Wilson worked for six dollars a week, and gave a dollar every Sunday to the church. He had a gruff voice, and there was just no way he could sing, so I had to lead the singing, lead prayer, and do just about everything. But the congregation grew gradually, and we were able to get a preacher later."

Faulkner had sung in the glee club in high school and at the University of Missouri, but he never considered himself a good singer. Still, he led the singing for his church for about fifty years.

"I don't do it anymore, because as you get older, your voice gets lower, and fortunately we have some very capable singers now.

When I started, I could hardly carry a tune. But there was this older lady, Aunt Mel Mashburn, who had what people call 'perfect pitch.' I would get her to sit on the front pew, and she would quietly start me off, and I would take it from there. I was about the only one who could hear her, but it was enough to give me the proper pitch," he laughs.

"The Bay Minette church of Christ has been expanded in the last five or six years by adding a two hundred thousand dollar fellowship hall and remodeling the inside of the main auditorium with new lights, new pews, and new decor. It is a beautiful interior and seats about two hundred."

Faulkner is faithful to the church. He serves as an elder, as church treasurer, and he taught Sunday School for more than forty years. The members are liberal givers, compared to their financial ability, but Faulkner has long been the largest contributor.

"I have strong beliefs and have a strong faith in God. I sincerely believe that His word is gospel, and that if we expect to go to Heaven, we must be obedient to His commands," Faulkner asserts.

When he was first married, his wife Evelyn had been the organist in the local Methodist church. Musical instruments such as organs and pianos are not used in worship services of the church of Christ. Was this difference hard to overcome?

"Well, we discussed it very much. But when she married me, she began attending the church of Christ, and she quit playing the organ in church. She did play for many weddings in the community. But for a long time, she never became a member. Four or five years later, when I was in the Army Air Corps, without my knowledge, she was baptized into the church of Christ.

"At the time, we were living in Pampa, Texas, where I was a pilot instructor. Evelyn knew that I knew what she ought to do. I never pushed or shoved or anything. Well, there was a revival being conducted there. She went one day and was baptized, and when I came home, she told me. Of course, I was delighted."

WHILE EACH CHURCH of Christ congregation is independent, they often cooperate in such areas as financing what they determine to be good causes. One of those "good causes" supported by members of the church of Christ is a Christian university in Montgomery. Over the years, Faulkner has been its biggest contributor and he served as chairman of its board for twenty-six years.

"Several times I had been asked to get active in Alabama Christian College and turned them down. Finally, in 1958, I was asked to meet in a Montgomery motel room with Dr. Rex Turner, founder of the college, Dr. V. P. Black, and Gus Nichols. They persuaded me to come on the board of directors, and that's where it started. As is often the case, I get too interested and too active," Faulkner smiles.

"The school has grown from fewer than two hundred students, from the time I was chosen to serve on the board, to about twenty-eight hundred at present. The university has a well-known and respected law school, the Jones School of Law, along with the regular courses you would expect to receive at a liberal arts college, including a master's degree in business.

"Every student is required to study the Bible and the school has a daily chapel where students are able to participate in prayer, singing and hearing enriching programs."

The acquisition of the Jones School of Law, a difficult endeavor, came from a Faulkner idea in 1983.

"It occurred to me that the University of Alabama, who owned the school, was not going to do anything with it. They had purchased it for seventy-five thousand dollars from Charlie Bennett so that no other public institution could have a law school in the capital city. I thought that perhaps the university would not mind a private Christian-oriented school owning it. In my mind, I was sure that they would not want Auburn, especially, or even Troy State or the University of South Alabama, to have a law school. Finally, I decided to talk with Dr. Joab Thomas, who was president at the time, to see if he might consider selling the law school. He told me he would think about it.

"I did not hear from Dr. Thomas for about two months. Finally, he called and said that the university was interested in selling it and asked, 'What will you give us for it?'

"I said, 'Dr. Thomas, I do not buy law schools every week, and I do not choose to put a price on your commodity except, I will pay you what you paid for it.'"

Thomas laughed, and stated it wasn't every week that he sold a law school, and said he would think about it further and get back with him.

About two months later, Thomas called Faulkner and said he would take two hundred and twenty-five thousand dollars for the law school.

"That's fine," Faulkner replied. "We'll pay you fifty thousand cash and the rest at twenty-five thousand dollars a year until it is paid for."

Thomas said he could not do that, that he must have the cash.

"Yes you can," Faulkner said, "because we'll pay you six percent interest."

Thomas agreed, and Faulkner contacted two lawyer friends in Huntsville to obtain the fifty thousand dollar down payment.

At first, there was some opposition to the law school purchase, but board members finally agreed to it.

"There were some church members over the state who thought the law school had no business being at a Christian university. My answer to them was, 'Well, lawyers need Christian education as badly as anyone I know,'" Faulkner smiled.

The law school now is self-supporting and has added considerable prestige to the university. Faulkner believes that in the long run, it will have more and more credibility and influence throughout the southeast, since it is the only law school connected with the churches of Christ east of Pepperdine in California.

"When we get the school accredited by the American Bar Association, which will be soon, we believe students will come from all over the country east of the Rocky Mountains. It has already grown from seventy-five students to more than four hundred," Faulkner added.

The new complex, which has just been completed, cost about ten million dollars, including law books.

Faulkner remembers that at one time, when the school was struggling financially, some board members wanted to sell the law school for about two and a half million dollars.

"I told the president that the law school was not going to be sold. I did not mean to be ugly, I just knew that the University of Alabama had put a clause in the sales contract that if we ever sold it, they would have the first opportunity to purchase it. I also knew that the Alabama Commission on Higher Education would never approve another law school in Alabama for a public institution."

IN 1983, THE BOARD of directors voted to change the name of Alabama Christian College to Faulkner University. Faulkner does not mention that the university itself would have been forced to close more than once for financial reasons had he not come to the rescue.

"One time it was a hundred and fifty thousand dollars. Another time, it was more than that. And still another time, it was just fifty thousand dollars. Contrary to what a lot of people think, I am not rich in money. You may find this difficult to believe, but it's the truth. When I graduated from college, I owed five hundred dollars that I had to borrow to get through the last year. Before I was twenty-one years old, I owed over twelve thousand dollars, and that was in 1936. That was a fortune in those days. And I have *never* been out of debt, and am not out of debt today. I've got assets that exceed what I owe, and enough insurance and so forth to pay whatever I owe. But with a little luck, I'll be out of debt this year or next, if I don't keep giving it away. But I have given away, I guess, four or five million dollars, always on borrowed money.

"It would be easy for me to say, 'Well, I can't help on this cause until I get out of debt,' but the Lord didn't put me in debt. I put myself in debt. So that's why I try to give a good portion of what I make to good causes. And, it's paid in the long run. I might would have had more money in the bank, but would have less other things."

Faulkner agrees that going into debt to give money away might sound foolish to some people. But he quickly turns to the scriptures.

"You see, giving is . . . I don't want to say it's a habit, but it becomes a habit. It's a pleasure. Jesus, for example, in Acts 20:35, is quoted as saying, 'It is more blessed to give than to receive.' And many scriptures in the Bible teach you that. Proverbs 11:25, 'The liberal soul shall be made fat, and he that waters shall be watered unto.' And in Luke 6:38, 'Give and it shall be given unto you; good measure, pressed down, shaken together, and running over, shall men give into your bosom.'

"So God says, if you give, you will be rewarded. Most people never realize that. They have never had the pleasure of doing it, but it's true. But you've got to believe it.

"I know that most people would say I'm a fool, but every dollar I've given to the university up there, and it's at least four million dollars, was borrowed money."

Did his family think he was foolish at the time he borrowed so much money and gave it to the university?

"They didn't know it. I'm sure they would have thought I was foolish, but they didn't know I had borrowed the money to give away. Even Evelyn, I never told her either. In fact, I don't know that I've ever told anybody before now." Faulkner concedes that he never confided his financial decisions in his wife because she would have worried, and he wanted to spare her those concerns.

"The point I'm getting to is this. Most people would say, and certainly my two sons would say, 'Daddy, you're in debt, and you're giving money away. That's foolish.' And to the average person, it is foolish. They'd say, 'why don't you get out of debt'?

"Well, look at it this way. Let's say I hadn't given the money. In the last ten years of inflation, the average increase in property and investments has been 20 percent a year. Well, say take that three million dollars, and it doubles. At 20 percent it doubles every forty-two months if you leave it all in there. I'd be worth fifteen million or twenty million dollars. But I feel that I'm richer than if I had twenty million dollars. Most people wouldn't feel that way," Faulkner says.

Faulkner feels he is richer because he has done a lot for people . . . he's done a lot of people good. He has helped educate a lot of kids. And if you want to put it on a practical basis that some other people might believe, as a result he has two colleges named for him. Is that worth anything? He thinks it's worth more to his posterity than having three or four million dollars. He feels that some day, it will be worth more to his family in pride.

Says Faulkner, "It's a matter of what you value. Of course, we all value money. But money is not the only thing to value. Money will not create happiness. The lack of it will create unhappiness, but having it will not create happiness. Just like Mr. Barber of Barber Dairies, who has millions and millions, said the other day, 'You know, I can't put any more ketchup or any more mustard on my hamburger.' So the pleasure in life, and I sincerely believe this, is not what you do for yourself. It's what you do for others. And I've gotten into a lot of trouble helping others, but I'm going to keep on trying. When I get to the point that I can't help other people, and help the Lord, I've got no further reason to be here. I'm just of no value like that.

"I would hate to walk around town and be worth fifteen million or twenty million, and couldn't think of anybody that I had helped, or any good that I had done."

"I've been very fortunate. I've made a lot of money, but I've given away a lot. I've never wished for money for the purpose of living luxuriously. I've always wanted to have money to give away. That's what I enjoy. My mother, I guess, taught me that."

Does Faulkner believe that by giving money to the university in Montgomery he is laying up treasures in Heaven?

"I surely do. You know, the only way you can lay up treasures in Heaven is to give it away. Think about it! You're not going to take it with you when you die. The only way you can get it up there is to give it away to some good purpose down here.

"Sometimes my conscience has hurt me in the past because I didn't become a preacher. But I have consoled myself in the feeling that I have helped to produce more preachers and done more good than if I had preached myself.

"Besides, I don't see how anybody could feel good about having more millions in the bank than they can intelligently use.

"And I may get out of debt this year," Faulkner smiles.

. . . the American man-at-arms. His name and fame
are the birthright of every American citizen. In his
youth and strength, his love and loyalty, he gave all
that mortality can give. He has never failed us. Were
he to do so, a million ghosts in olive drab, in brown
khaki, in blue and gray, would rise up from their white
crosses thundering those magic words: Duty, Honor,
Country!

General Douglas MacArthur
May 12, 1962, address at the
United States Military Academy

8

Duty, Honor, Country

It was a cool Sunday afternoon on December 7, 1941. As on nearly every other Sunday before this one, Jimmy Faulkner had attended church and was enjoying a restful afternoon lying in bed, listening to his little radio. It was before the debut of television, and families throughout America relied heavily on radio for both entertainment and news coverage.

Suddenly, the regular program was interrupted with a news bulletin. Blaring over his radio speaker, as through radio sets nationwide, came the stunning news that the Japanese had attacked Pearl Harbor. The unbelievable event would drastically change the future of the country, as well as the hopes and dreams of American citizens everywhere.

In the weeks and months to follow, young men and women who grew up in the Great Depression would now put aside their personal plans and simple expectations to fight a war in places with strange-sounding names they had never heard. Young men who had plowed the hard clay of cotton fields and had never seen the ocean would enlist in the Navy to sail the high seas. Boys fresh out of high school who had never seen an airplane up close would stand in line to volunteer for pilot training. Others, by the hundreds of thousands, were ready to ship off to basic training to learn how to fight in Uncle Sam's army, hand-to-hand if necessary, to defend their country with honor.

It was a time that would draw deeply upon the rich patriotism in the hearts of Americans everywhere, and cause families to rely even more upon their steadfast faith in God to help them cope with separation from loved ones and the constant danger of foreign battlefields.

The moods and the emotions of the people of Bay Minette, as in most small towns in America, were mixed. They were worried, excited, concerned, and puzzled. Who would believe that the Japanese were foolish enough to jump on Uncle Sam? But what you did not hear or see were protests. There was no dissent. Americans would stand united, heart to heart, arm in arm, to defend to the death, if necessary, their great country.

In terms of lives lost and material destruction, it would become the most devastating war in human history. The United States alone would eventually mobilize some sixteen million people for military service and the monetary cost would soar to an estimated $341 billion. American citizens, wealthy and poor alike, would be asked to ration war-needed materials and to purchase United States Savings Bonds to help underwrite the unprecedented expense. It would be another sixty years before Americans would be so motivated, and that would result from an attack on our own soil by terrorists who would crash our own airline carriers into the twin towers of the World Trade Center in New York and the Pentagon on September 11, 2001.

Faulkner, then responsible for providing for his young wife and two small boys, was eager to do whatever he could for his country. He got his chance one morning when political acquaintance Marc

Ray "Foots" Clement, who had helped elect U.S. Senators John Sparkman and Lister Hill, asked him to serve as deputy director of the state's volunteer effort to sell war savings bonds.

"I spent three or four days a week, in and out of Birmingham, promoting the sale of bonds. I had a part-time editor who helped with the *Times*. I was selling war bonds and helping organize the effort statewide," Faulkner recalls.

The bond effort, while greatly successful, also fueled the young publisher's allegiance to his country.

"When you're talking to people about war bonds, the patriotism kind of gets to you. Finally, my heart and mind indicated to me that I had to do more. I was perfectly healthy and just felt compelled to enlist.

"I didn't have to go. In the first place, I was a newspaperman. Next, I had a wife and two children. I just felt it was my duty. I discussed it with Evelyn. She didn't want me to go, but she didn't object. And fortunately, I was able to get somebody to take over the newspaper."

Faulkner resigned as mayor, which he did not regret as he already had served more than two years, enough time to be bothered with the problems and worries of a small town. He leased the *Baldwin Times* to Ford Cook at $150 a month. Then he joined the Army Air Corps.

Faulkner was shipped off to Texas to the San Antonio Air Center for a ten-week training program. His glee club experience and time spent directing the music at church would come in handy.

"They made us sing when we were marching. Songs like, 'Dinah Won't You Blow Your Horn.' That was one of the most popular marching songs because it had a good rhythm to it. And there were others.

"They had a barber shop there, and the first thing they did was shave your head. I remember when I was sitting there in the barber's chair they were playing the song, 'That Old Black Magic,' on the record player. I can hear it now. It's strange how songs like that remind you of various things. Songs like Kate Smith's 'Carolina Moon.' There are not many moon songs anymore. And then, 'When the Moon Shines Over the Mountain'; I learned that one as a young boy going out to New Mexico," Faulkner reminisced.

"But after we got to flying, we didn't have time to sing. We had to concentrate on what we were doing."

From basic training, Faulkner was transferred to Sikeston, Missouri, for private flight training where he would first fly solo, then begin intensive training as a pilot. His next stop would land him in Coffeeville, Kansas, and his first close brush with death.

"We were flying a PT-13, and Lieutenant Rodgers was my instructor. He was sitting in the back seat and I was in the front. I remember that the ceiling was about eighteen hundred feet that day, and we were flying at about fifteen hundred feet. My instructor decided to put me through a forced landing. He cut the engine, pulled back the throttle, and left me to find a field in which to land. Luckily, I spotted a pasture below pretty fast. I was supposed to take the plane down to about a hundred feet and the instructor would take over, put the throttle on, go around, and turn it back to me.

"I was lucky and hit the approach to the field pretty good, but when he put the throttle to it, we had a dead engine. Fortunately, he hit the field, about the last one-third of it, and we probably were on the ground about a couple of hundred feet and were headed straight for a tree. At the last minute, he swerved the airplane to the side, but it knocked the wing off. Fortunately, neither of us was hurt seriously. I got an injured elbow."

As Faulkner walked away from the wrecked airplane, he remembered that twelve cadets prior to this accident had been killed in similar incidents. "It was an amazing thing. I was about 150 feet above the ground, and of course I knew what had happened. It's unbelievable how much of my life went through my mind in the next six or seven seconds . . . my family, my children that I had left behind . . . the Lord. You think of so many things. And of course, you have time to pray."

What caused the accident?

"Back then, you had carburetors that would vaporize with moisture and, with the ceiling that low, vapor got into it," Faulkner concluded.

The experience was the first of three close calls for the new pilot.

AT COFFEEVILLE, Faulkner had been able to rent a room so that his family could join him. They accompanied him now as he transferred to Pampa, Texas, for advanced pilot training, where the young pilot would learn to handle the large B-25 bombers. He had not done too well in the single-engine aircraft, but at Pampa, it was a different story. When he got to multi-engines, he rated superior in his flying, which was unusual for a second lieutenant. His handling of the complicated bomber qualified him well for what he had assumed would be overseas duty. What he had not realized was that the best pilots were kept as instructors.

"It was supposed to be a compliment, so I guess I was flattered. And at the time, I was glad to be chosen as an instructor because my family had joined me and I knew I could be with them for a number of months.

"But it was pretty rough. I would get up about 3 o'clock in the morning to go to the flight line. Evelyn would always get up and cook me a big breakfast because I would not get back down until around 1:30 or 2. She would cook eggs and biscuits, and after breakfast she would go back to bed until the kids got up," he remembered.

As an instructor at Pampa, he had his second close call.

"I was sitting in the right seat of the B-25 with a student in the left seat and another student in the back. I would go up and fly with one for an hour, land the plane, and the students would change seats and we would go through the procedures again.

"This one morning it was cold and the snow was everywhere. The student was taking off and, all of a sudden, I noticed that we were hardly off the ground but the air speed was barely one hundred miles per hour. The stalling speed was about that. Well, I took over and hollered, 'Mayday!'

"In an emergency situation like this, we were taught to land straight ahead because a plane will stall out faster if you turn. But there were treacherous mountains and valleys straight ahead, and I knew that if we kept going straight, it meant sure death.

"I was able to get the speed up to 105 miles an hour and, very cautiously, I eased it around slowly until eventually it was lined up with a runway. Of course, all the fire trucks came out for the emergency landing and just when we were about five feet off the ground, the tower yelled, 'Wheels!' I hadn't been thinking about wheels; I was just thinking about getting back on that field. So I flipped it down, and the wheels came down at the same time I hit the ground. I was lucky. I could not see that smoke was coming out of the engines, because they were a little behind me.

"At the time, I had no idea what was wrong. After I got on the ground, the major called me in and talked to me. After I told him what had happened, I learned that, because of the freezing weather, the ground crew had put gasoline in the oil to keep it from freezing. The mechanic is supposed to run the engine fifteen minutes before takeoff to burn that out, but he had not done that. If I had known that, maybe I could have stayed up there another ten minutes and it would have burned off and I would have been all right. But I didn't know," Faulkner said.

The students marveled at their instructor's calmness and came to him after it was all over and said, "Lieutenant, you didn't even get excited."

However, Faulkner was not able to hide his private apprehensions from the military dentist sometime later. The dentist noted that while the instructor appeared to be reserved and calm, his teeth told a different story. They were worn from constant "gritting" during tense situations.

"I can tell you aren't calm," the captain-dentist noted. "Inwardly, I can tell that you get excited."

It was a problem Faulkner had to deal with.

"When I first became an instructor, I would catch myself being so excited, landing and everything. You've got to trust these students, and make them think you trust them, coming in there at 110 miles per hour to hit the ground.

"I've even had students get so excited they would turn the engines off in the air. But I made up my mind that I had to get over that nervousness, and I did."

THE THIRD CLOSE CALL came on the final night of one of Faulkner's classes.

"We had eight students per class. I had a couple of students who only lacked a few minutes of flying time, and it was night. We always kept a red light down near our feet so that we could see the instruments. One of the students was flying and I stooped over to pick up this light. My eyes left the horizon for just an instant. When I looked up, this other B-25 was coming right toward us, right at the same level. I thought he was within fifty feet of us. I slammed the control forward, and just went right under him. Luckily he did not hit my tail. He was in the wrong place, but that would not have kept him from killing us," Faulkner recalls.

Faulkner realized that pilot instructor duties were far more dangerous than an overseas assignment.

"They lost many more pilots in the training command than they did overseas. I guess maybe three or four times as many. In Kansas, there was a young boy from Montgomery who was on the runway, waiting to take off, and was struck from behind by another cadet who could not see him, because you could not see right in front of you in that type airplane. You had to taxi from side to side.

"Then, I had another friend from Ohio, a fine-looking young man, who was killed in a forced landing, similar to the one when my plane crashed."

Faulkner was instructor for five classes of eight students each. He lost two of his own forty students in fatal crashes.

"I had a brilliant, nineteen-year-old boy who I soloed after about four hours. Another instructor had a student who was pretty equal to mine, so we put them into a brand new B-25. My cadet was the pilot first. One would log pilot time, the other co-pilot time, then they would land and swap. As quickly as my cadet got into the air, he headed for Enid, Oklahoma. It was probably 150 miles away, and out of our assigned flying area. He had gone there to buzz his girlfriend's farm home. The plane hit a windmill on the farm, killing both cadets and destroying the new B-25.

"Another of my cadets lacked only fifteen minutes of flying time. His wife and two kids had come to celebrate his receiving his wings. The captain of my squadron saw that he lacked just a few minutes, and since this was the final night, he took him and another cadet out to complete their time. They never came back and I don't know what happened to them. Fortunately for me, someone else had to break the sad news to the cadet's wife."

Pampa, Texas, also provided some of the earliest childhood memories of Faulkner's oldest son, Jimmy, who entered the first grade there. Several weeks later, knowing that another transfer was in the offing, Evelyn took the boys back to Alabama where they would stay temporarily with Faulkner's brother, Thurston, and his wife, Odette.

Faulkner was slated for duty at Liberal, Kansas, when he learned that several in his unit were headed for Courtland, Alabama. He persuaded his commander to change his orders so that he could return to his home state and again have his family with him. After finding a place to stay, Faulkner sent for his family to join him in Decatur.

The young lieutenant spent thirteen weeks transition time, logging hours in the bulky B-24 bombers, before being transferred to Harlingen, Texas. There, Faulkner would continue his training in preparation for combat action in the B-29.

One day at Harlingen, Faulkner noticed there were three B-25's on the flight line for administrative purposes. Quickly, he volunteered his services as a pilot, should one be needed. A few days later, he was asked to fly one of the B-25's to Miami to pick up Colonel Roy T. Wright, the base commander. As a result of a communications foul-up, Faulkner landed at a different airport from the one where the Colonel was waiting. Faulkner waited a day-and-a-half while Wright was pacing the floor at a different airport looking for his pilot. Wright finally checked things out and located his crew and airplane late in the day, too late to begin the flight.

Early the next morning Faulkner and his co-pilot, a lieutenant, headed back to Harlingen with the colonel. They were in the air only a few minutes when Faulkner asked the co-pilot to fill out "Form One," a required procedure for all such flights.

After looking, the co-pilot reported to his pilot that there was no such form aboard the airplane. Faulkner then began to circle back to the airport and assigned the lieutenant the task of informing their commander of the mishap. Meanwhile, Faulkner called the flight tower to have the form ready when they landed.

On their second take-off, Colonel Wright decided he wanted to be co-pilot. Faulkner kept waiting for the colonel to chew him out, but it never happened on the return flight. He thought perhaps Wright would assign that task to some other officer after they returned.

The next day, after Faulkner returned from routine flight training, he was notified to report to the commanding officer. As he entered Wright's office, he saw his personnel file on the colonel's desk. His commander commented on the fact that Faulkner had been mayor of Bay Minette, then also noted that he was a member of Kappa Alpha fraternity at the University of Missouri.

"I was KA too," the commander commented.

"How would you like to be assigned as my assistant?" the colonel asked.

Faulkner was lost for words. Instead of being reprimanded, he was being promoted to the highly desired position of assistant adjutant.

Faulkner wondered how Wright thought about looking at his record and decided he never would have, had Faulkner not screwed up in Miami.

It was some time later that he learned that Wright's adjutant, Captain Clifton Kirkpatrick from Selma, Alabama, had put Faulkner's records on the colonel's desk. Kirkpatrick had discovered that he and Faulkner had many mutual friends, most of them political, and making Faulkner assistant adjutant had been Kirkpatrick's idea.

A few months later, Wright got his orders to go overseas and was replaced by a West Point graduate, Colonel Hughes.

"Colonel Hughes had just returned from his overseas duty and he found out that I knew Lister Hill and John Sparkman. The Central Flying Training Command was headquartered at Maxwell, yet we were at Harlingen. Colonel Hughes arranged to get the commanding general of Maxwell to Harlingen and also arranged to have me in his audience. Hughes wanted me to be the general's aide, and the general selected me.

"Well, that would have been a big honor a year or two before, but at that time, I knew the war wasn't going to last that much longer, and I didn't want to be a general's aide," Faulkner remembered.

Like most young men in the forties, Faulkner had been eager to enlist and do his part for his country. But with the war now ending, he was equally eager to return home to his family and resume his civilian life.

The military began discharging personnel by service numbers. Faulkner's adjutant friend from Selma, Cliff Kirkpatrick, knew of the lieutenant's situation, and of his desire to return home. One day, when the colonel was out of town, a telegram came through from headquarters with several numbers for discharge.

"I called the sergeant who was in charge of personnel and said, 'Sergeant, is one of those numbers mine?' He said, 'No, lieutenant, yours is a long way from that.' About thirty or forty minutes later the sergeant called back and said, 'Lieutenant, I made a mistake. One of those numbers is yours.'

"By the time the colonel could get back from out of town, I had cleared the field and got a B-25 set aside and a lieutenant to fly with me to Atlanta for discharge. I was out of the army and in Bay Minette by the time the colonel got back, and boy did he raise cain,"

Faulkner exclaimed. Faulkner realized that had the colonel been on base, the orders would have been canceled, and there was no telling when he would have gotten out of military service.

About a month before his discharge, Faulkner received a letter from Cook, the man who had taken charge of the *Baldwin Times*, saying he would have to give up the paper. Cook, who was disabled and could not serve in the military, had the *Times* running smoothly and apparently had done quite well for himself. The timing was perfect as Faulkner returned to Bay Minette before Cook had to leave.

The Faulkner family settled back into their modest, two-bedroom home on East Fifth Street, happy to be back home.

9

Family Matters

When Jimmy Faulkner, Jr., started school in the first grade, his father was in the Army Air Corps. He and his younger brother, Wade, demanded much of their mother's time and energy as Evelyn would strive to provide a home environment as the family moved from place to place, trying to spend as much time as possible with the children's pilot father.

"Jimmy Junior," as he was destined to be called well into his adult life, has obscured memories of his father during the early years.

"Of course, I didn't get to see a lot of him. I started the first grade in Pampa, Texas, then moved to Auburn, Alabama, where we lived with Daddy's brother, as Dad was being moved to Courtland Air Base near Decatur. We later moved there when he was able to get us a place in which to live. So my first year I went to school in Pampa, Texas, Auburn, and Decatur, Alabama. Before we moved to Pampa, Daddy was taking his basic training in Coffeeville, Kansas, where the Dalton Brothers had their killing."

One memory of the war era that stood out in the young boy's mind was the death of President Roosevelt.

"I remember that I was getting a haircut and somebody came running in and said F.D.R. had died. You know, they always say you remember something like that by where you were when you heard about it. I remember all the women crying, and everything."

At the same time, Jimmy's father had heard the sad news on the radio.

"I was riding in from the airport with fellow lieutenants from Courtland, Alabama, to Decatur when it came over the radio that he had died. Tears actually came to my eyes, as well as the other aviators. I well remember his 'Fireside Chats' in which he would bring us up to date about various and sundry things. This was before television, and he always had great radio audiences. We who were in the Air Corps at the time felt lifted up from the encouragement he gave all of us."

Roosevelt, who was president when Japan bombed Pearl Harbor, never lived to see the end of the war. He died of a cerebral hemorrhage at Warm Springs, Georgia, on April 12, 1945.

Wade was too young to remember the war as he was born less than a year before it started. His childhood memories are pleasant ones.

"I was always happy. I don't remember any disruption. I guess I was lucky."

Faulkner's military service and his later involvement in the political arena would require travel and time away from his home and family. Balancing family and career demands would present a challenge.

"When I was gone during the week, and off and on I was, I made it a point all during my career to spend Saturday and Sunday with my family. Very seldom would I be gone on the weekend. Of course, during the campaigns I was gone a lot, but Evelyn was with me a lot, and the boys were with me some.

"I was gone more than I would like to have been, and if I had it to do over again, I imagine I would have done it a little differently, I don't know, because I like close families. But I made sure I was with the family most of the time."

However, older son Jimmy felt his father was away from home too much.

When questioned about the early memories of his father, his expression becomes morose.

"You know, I always remember him being gone.

"First, he was in the service. As soon as he got out of service, he ran for the Democratic Executive Committee and he went with George Wallace to the national convention when the Dixiecrats walked out. Then he did a lot of traveling when he started running for state senator, and when he was elected he was gone a lot, although Wade and I took turns being pages. One week I would be page in Montgomery, and the next week it would be Wade's turn.

"Then, he started running for governor in the fifties, and I was going to school at Indian Springs (near Birmingham) at the time, in the ninth, tenth, and eleventh grades. I came home in the summer and the three big holidays, spring break, Thanksgiving, and Christmas. You know, I just wasn't around him much during that time. He would come by when he was campaigning up there, maybe carry me out to eat or something like that.

"It was during this time that Dad founded Loyal American Life Insurance Company in Mobile and worked there, although he would come home every night.

"Then the next four years, he spent a lot of time campaigning and he was gone a lot. I was at Marion Institute during the next election. Then I went to the University of Alabama.

"So, you know, during my formative years he was gone or I was away from home. We had some time together, but not a whole lot.

Some during the summertime. Then in the sixties when Wallace was doing all his running for president, of course I was a little older, but Dad was gone to California some of the time.

"I remember doing things with my mother, like when Wade went to Europe on a Boy Scout Jamboree, Mother and I went up to New York to meet him on the boat but Daddy was gone. We just accepted that fact."

For Wade, it was a different story. The absence of his father was no serious issue.

"I never recall it being a problem. He usually showed up on Saturday and Sunday, and we always went to church when he was there. Sometimes, if he was not there, we might not go, but he was usually there."

For Wade, having a popular father involved in politics was a matter of pride.

"There was always somebody new and interesting showing up at the dinner table. I mean, a wide variety of politicians, U.S. Senators, governors, musicians, authors, artists, and doctors. There was always somebody interesting. I learned to listen back then. I wouldn't say much, but I would sit there and listen. As a kid, I always took pride in telling people my daddy was a newspaper man. I didn't know what an editor was, but I knew he was a newspaper man," Wade recalls.

The younger son also enjoyed his stint as a page in the Alabama Senate.

"I was ten or eleven, and that's when I started driving. On Monday morning, I would drive him to Montgomery while he read whatever he had to read. We stayed at the Whitley Hotel, and we would come back every Thursday or Friday. But back then, it was only every other year and the sessions did not last very long."

One of Wade's favorite memories was that of his mother

playing the piano. "She played a lot, especially in my grammar school years, and some later in my high school years until she had arthritis. She also wrote poetry for awhile for her own pleasure, but she was pretty good at it. Mother was very supportive. She always made sure I got my Cub Scout projects done and my homework done. She was a loving, sweet person," Wade remembers.

Brother Jimmy agrees, and says he was influenced in his early years more by his mother.

"We were with Mother most of the time. We would take trips, and sometimes Daddy would take us on a trip. Like going hunting. He carried me hunting several times, and fishing maybe six or eight times.

"But Mother pretty much made us study. When it came to discipline, she could be talked out of things a lot easier than Daddy could. She would take our sides a lot of times. Daddy wasn't all that strict, except certain things like going to church. When Sunday came around, you went to church! And Sunday night you went to church, regardless what else was going on. And Wednesday, too! It wasn't any use talking about it. Going to church was one thing we were going to do. I don't care what ball game or something else was going on, you went to church. Even when we were traveling, we would find a church of Christ, and we'd go to church," Jimmy Jr. recalls.

And while Jimmy felt his father was away from home often, he harbors pleasant memories of his earliest years in their first home.

"It was a small house with maybe two closets in the whole house. Everybody used chifforobes back then. We had in this old house an attic with disappearing stairway that came down in the hall. Daddy had some of the attic floored so they could store things. But I remember Wade and I used to build model airplanes, and we would go up there on a rainy day and you could hear the rain coming down on the roof. We had a table set up to make our model airplanes, and we would read funnybooks. That was a big thing back then, and kids would come over to the house and we would trade funnybooks and go up in the attic. And everything was just peaceful," Jimmy Jr. added.

The boys' father singles out a special memory of his sons' youth.

"I still have a vivid memory of the happy moment when the two boys looked out the kitchen window and spotted a small pony. Their faces glowed and they could hardly wait to run out and see what Flicker looked like. I had built the horse a fence and small barn. Many times they would come from over toward the high school, one riding, one by the side of Flicker, with their white dog, Rustler, holding on to Flicker's tail. I wish I had a picture of this," Faulkner recalls.

The senior Faulkner would one day see one of his prayers answered. "I was very anxious for my own children to be members of the church. One day while I was leading singing, both of my sons came forward to be baptized. This was one of the most thrilling moments in my life.

"Coincidentally, about eighteen years later, I was again leading singing and both of my grandsons, Jim, III, and Henry Wade, came forward under similar circumstances."

His sons, Wade and Jimmy, are great friends today, but it was not always that way. Growing up, they had their typical childhood spats, as Wade remembers.

"Of course, Jimmy was older than me in high school, and he went off to Indian Springs, but we never got along very well. We fussed and scraped, and he went off to Alabama to college. And I'm pretty sure that's the reason I went to Auburn the first year, just because he went to Alabama.

"Then my girlfriend, Ann, came on to Auburn, and music is her life. At that time Auburn's music department was not that outstanding, so she was in psychology, or something like that. It just occurred to me that we ought to transfer to Alabama, so we did. I roomed with Jimmy his last year at Alabama, and we've gotten along beautifully ever since," Wade said.

> I've never known a dog to wag
> His tail in glee he did not feel,
> Nor quit his old-time friend to tag
> At some more influential heel.
> The yellowest cur I ever knew
> Was to the boy who loved him true.
> I've never known a dog to show
> Halfway devotion to his friend;
> To seek a kinder man to know,
> Or richer; but unto the end
> The humblest dog I ever knew
> was to the man that loved him true.
> Anonymous

DOGS PROVED TO BE the favorite pets for members of the Faulkner family. Faulkner remembers that he was not as fortunate when he was a small boy and times were hard.

"My father would not let us have dogs, stating they ate too much. He preferred feeding the scraps to the hogs. He did allow a cat or two around the farm to catch mice and rats. Finally, when I was about ten, he let me have a terrier, which was a four-eyed Indian dog. That meant he had two eyes and a brown spot over each eye. He was a small dog, but I named him Jumbo. He was supposed to catch rats, but he was better at eating biscuits than anything else.

If he ever caught a rat, it never became known to my father since he was kind of critical of the biscuits he did eat. However, Jumbo and I were great friends and we played a lot together.

"When my father died and I had to leave the farm, I gave Jumbo to my first cousin, Charles Greer, who also lived on a farm across Yellow Creek. Charles had a much bigger dog, named Carlo, which was a fine squirrel, 'possum and 'coon dog, and he managed to teach Jumbo a few of the things about being a hunting dog. Charles and I were great friends and I would go over and spend weekends with him and we would go hunting or fishing and some nights my uncle would take us 'possum hunting," Faulkner recalls.

The companionship of a dog was a pleasure that would not be denied his sons. In fact, Wade never remembers a time when he did not have a dog. One of his favorite memories is his long friendship with Max.

"He was a big Dalmatian. I had him from the time I was in the fourth grade until I graduated from high school. He was a good buddy. He went to school with me every day, and even went into the classroom with me and he would lie down under my desk. I don't know how the teachers tolerated it, but they did."

Max did not receive a diploma as he had to drop out of school in the middle of the eleventh grade. Another boy in the class insisted that he be allowed to also bring his dog to school. Unfortunately, the two canines met in the school library and the amorous event was too much distraction for the students.

Faulkner's son, Jimmy, remembers a white mixed-breed named Rustler, a constant companion that spent the nights with them inside the small, two-bedroom home on Fifth Street.

"We had one bath, no air conditioning, a floor furnace and space heaters. I don't ever remember it being hot, but I remember being cold because there was no heat in the bedroom. When we went to bed at night in the winter, it was just like running outside to bed.

"It was cold, and we had this floor furnace, and the bedroom doors and the bathroom door opened up into this hallway. Well, Daddy would sit out in this little hallway where the floor furnace was to read the paper. Mother used to always get onto him for throwing the paper on the floor when he would finish.

"One night after we all had gone to bed, the paper caught on fire and was burning. Rustler started howling and knocked the door open somehow, and woke Daddy up. I was about nine and Wade was about six, and I remember standing there with Wade, and the flames were flaring up. Mother threw a wet wash rag on it, and of course the rag burned up too. The kitchen was way around the corner in the other part of the house but the bathroom was right next to where the fire was. But Daddy kept running way around to the kitchen to get water and bring it back to throw on the fire. I'll never forget. Wade and I were just standing there watching him make trips back and forth when he could have gotten water from the bathroom which was right by the fire. All it did was smoke damage, because it was nothing but paper, but we all say that Rustler saved our lives."

The incident was an exciting, if not entertaining, event the boys would long remember. At the time, they did not realize that a freak house fire had taken the life of the grandfather they had never known and created the nightmare their father would live with throughout his life.

In later years, dogs would continue to be companions for the elder Faulkner. A golden retriever named Rusty was for years a favorite playmate of his eight grandchildren and a close companion on Faulkner's long walks in the neighborhood.

The last dog to live at the Faulkner residence was also a golden retriever. She was four months old upon arrival and was named "Missy."

"About two weeks after I got Missy, Don Siegelman called me and said, 'Jimmy, I've got a golden retriever puppy for you.'

"I thanked him and told him that another friend had given me one, and I turned it down. He didn't tell me he was going to be governor some day," Faulkner laughed.

"Missy was very obedient. She would walk with me over to the Forest Park area. The first time I took her, when she was old enough to walk with me, we stopped in at my Aunt Anabel Coleman's home. We went inside, and although she was some ninety years old, she got down on the floor with Missy and spent about thirty minutes training her. She taught her how to sit, to shake hands, to go and to come. That's all the training she ever had. After that, she was always obedient to that training," Faulkner remembered.

Missy lived a normal life span. After his walking companion died, Faulkner gave up his neighborhood strolls in favor of walking almost two miles daily on a machine inside his home in the early mornings.

> If you can start the day without caffeine,
> If you can get going without pep pills,
> If you can resist complaining and boring people with your troubles,
> If you can eat the same food every day and be grateful for it,
> If you can understand when your loved ones are too busy to give you any time,
> If you can overlook it when something goes wrong through no fault of yours and those you love take it out on you,

If you can take criticism and blame without resentment,
If you can ignore a friend's limited education
and never correct him,
If you can resist treating a rich friend better than a poor
friend,
If you can face the world without lies and deceit,
If you can conquer tension without medical help,
If you can relax without liquor,
If you can sleep without the aid of drugs,
If you can say honestly that deep in your heart you have
no prejudice against creed, color, religion or politics,
Then my friend, you are almost as good as your dog.

From a Florida Church Bulletin

WHAT KEEPS JIMMY FAULKNER awake at night? "My every night prayer is that my family be Christians. This has caused me much worry and loss of sleep. Don't misunderstand me. My descendants, including my sons, grandsons, great-grandsons and other children, have always been law-abiding citizens, never causing any trouble, never getting into any trouble such as dope, drinking, and as I recall, only one of my grandchildren even smoke."

Concerning his two sons, Faulkner has tried to be even-handed in their upbringing.

"I tried to treat them both fairly. During those early days when I first came to Bay Minette my one desire was to please my mother. When my sons were born, and after she died, I did things to please my family, particularly my two boys. However, I have often had the feeling that somehow or another I have not always pleased them.

"I've been very fortunate. I've always wanted to have money to give away. That's what I enjoy. Not many people feel that way. My mother, I guess, taught me that.

"She would not take insurance because she didn't want my brother and me to have anything when she died. She didn't want to leave any money. When she died, she had enough to pay for her funeral and doctor's bills and nineteen dollars in the bank. She wouldn't have wanted it any other way. The important thing to her was for us to have an education."

And does Faulkner believe this is a good philosophy?

"Oh yeah. I surely do. I feel little financial obligation to my grandchildren, for example, and I don't feel much of an obligation to my children because each of them has made more money than I have. And because they haven't given as much away, they are probably worth more than I am."

"When my grandchildren graduated from high school, I gave each an automobile, or the equivalent," Faulkner said. "And of course, I would give them anything I have now if they really needed it, but they all are doing well," he said.

Faulkner contends it is more important to provide children an education and an opportunity, rather than financial wealth.

"I gladly spent what it took to get Wade a doctor's degree, and it was rather expensive. He got married in college, and had children, and I gave him enough money for that — borrowed money — but he didn't know it was borrowed.

"And Jimmy, I paid for his education and arranged to let him have half interest in my newspaper business. I intended, if I died, to leave the newspaper business to him. I felt at the time that Wade was well protected, taken care of, and I thought it would be even. But the newspaper business went well, and when we sold them, to put it bluntly, Jimmy was a millionaire before he was thirty years old. And I felt that was adequate. And he's smart, he's done well financially," Faulkner said.

"Jimmy has very good common sense, and he's more conservative than I am, and he's probably made more money than I have. Wade has made more money than I have. Quite honestly, they think more in those areas. They have little interest in Faulkner University, for example, and I am sure that they feel like I have wasted a lot of my time. I don't know. They haven't told me that, but they have never indicated much interest in it. Each has given money to Faulkner University, however. After I die, they may be interested in it, I don't know. But I am sure that they feel I waste a lot of my time in civic activities.

"And Wade, he's practicing medicine, he's a member of the Rotary Club, but he's never been active in many of the things I've been interested in. And Jimmy is liberal in his giving, and I don't know whether Wade is or not. Jimmy is not liberal to the extent that I've always been liberal, but I'd say he's not stingy. He's been liberal with his children and has made a very good parent, as has Wade. But I just kind of have the feeling that Jimmy thinks I probably could have devoted my time to more worthwhile things, but I could be entirely wrong."

While Wade did better in school and has become a renowned opthamologist, a specialist in cataract and laser refractive surgery, Faulkner credits his older son, Jimmy, with being extremely smart, and a better businessman than his father. Jimmy does not totally disagree with his father.

"You know, I went with the newspaper and worked, and Daddy was the publisher and had an office there, but he was gone a lot then. That was in the sixties, and Wallace was doing all his campaigning, so he spent a lot of time in California and different places.

"He wrote the editorials, but the day-to-day business from about 1960 on, I did. But even though he was not involved in the daily operation of the business, he was there in case I had questions, and I would talk to him a lot about how he handled things, and he helped. But I had to make sure the money was there for the payroll. He had an office there and he was available for any problem we had, and he was overseeing the radio stations, but he was off with Wallace a lot," Jimmy added.

Did Jimmy ever share his father's interest in politics?

"Absolutely not! Of course, I'm interested in keeping up with politics, but personally, as far as running for something, Never! I was turned off politics. I look for a reason not to go to a meeting or gathering of people. I go when I have to, if I think I should be there. But if I don't have to be there, I'm going to miss it.

"I like going into a restaurant and nobody recognizes me. But last Friday, Beverly and I went to this restaurant in Mobile, and Daddy was with this group of people, and he's just always that way. Daddy likes an audience. Wherever he goes, you will see him with people. When he talks of eating alone, he's talking about with his wife.

"And I enjoy that. I enjoy not having to put up a front, or being nice to somebody, and my wife and I take trips just by ourselves and we enjoy it. But he's not going to do that. When they take a trip somewhere, there are two or three couples, always.

"No, politics, I just don't have any interest in it and still don't understand anybody doing it. But somebody's got to do it. And knowing what I know about it, I admire somebody who will do it and maintain integrity while they are in office, rather than suc- cumb to the winner's syndrome of only being interested in being re-elected and making a name for themselves.

"But even though you are able to do people favors, you don't like them camped at your doors, wanting you to do something for them. I just don't like the public exposure. You know, being jerked up during the campaign, my brother and I had to go over here and smile, like an idiot or something, while everybody is standing around. And they would ask you questions. But you know, some campaign person would tell us that 'if they ask this question, this is a good answer.' I was uneasy with the whole thing, and my brother, I feel, is the same way," Jimmy offered.

Wade agrees.

"I like to read about it in the newspapers, but not get involved in it. Only to the extent of giving donations to various candidates, but no more than that," Wade assures.

After the newspapers were sold, the older son became involved in several other businesses but now spends his time primarily in real estate development.

Both boys remain good friends.

"We don't have much social contact, being in different cities, but every now and then we'll go out and eat together, or go off hunting. We'll do that once or twice a year, or go fishing, or something like that. We're good friends, but he's so busy," says Jimmy.

Wade concedes that his practice keeps him extremely busy, but he loves his work.

"I enjoy leisure time, but I like to go to work. I have never regretted going into the field I am in. I never wake up in the morning wishing I didn't have to go to work," he says.

Wade traces his interest in becoming a doctor to his childhood, and to one of the many visitors to sit at the family dinner table.

"It started in our dining room, as did so many things. Over the years we have had some interesting people to come through our house to visit Daddy. One friend, way back, was Dr. Alston Callahan, who at the time was the Chairman of the Department of Ophthalmology at the Medical School of Alabama. He was very prominent nationally, and at that time wrote a lot of books. He later took me to the operating room with him up in Birmingham to see him do eye surgery.

"Even though I worked as a printer's devil, helping put out the weekly newspaper when I was nine or ten years old, I always thought that I wanted to be a doctor.

"I got married in college when I was nineteen to my nursery school sweetheart. I know my dad was very supportive of that. Looking back now at how ridiculous it might have seemed, I was still in school and she was in school and we decided to get married. He was supportive and supported me. As naive as I was, I didn't realize the significance to that. I do now. I am appreciative of it. I guess that was the best thing, or one of the best things, he ever did for me. Because it was so important to me.

"Looking back, Ann and I don't remember not knowing each other. Here we were in college, and it seemed like the thing to do, to get married. And it made all the difference. We didn't have much, but we didn't know we didn't have everything. But it made my grades take off. As an undergraduate, on a three point scale, I was having about a 2.4 before we got married. Then, I had about a 2.8 or 2.9. Then when I got to medical school, I went to the top of the class. I just got focused, and it just seemed easy. But being settled, and being supported by my family, I had no worries. I looked at going to school as my job, and getting the work done," Wade remembers.

Jimmy is proud of his brother's success.

"I admire him. He's done real well in his profession. It pleases me to hear people brag on him. He's real dedicated. In school, he wasn't satisfied with a C, which suited me fine. He always wanted an A, and most times he did make A's. He was tops in his medical class for three or four years. He's still dedicated. He's real brilliant."

Actually, Wade skipped his senior year in college and went

directly to medical school. He won the Dean's Award for having the highest four-year average at the University of Alabama School of Medicine.

Does Jimmy wish he had chosen a different career for himself?

"You know, I guess everybody goes through this, but when I was in college I wasn't interested in learning anything. I was interested in passing and getting out of college. Looking back on it now, I don't know if my life would have been any better, but I wish that, since I got into the newspaper business, I would have gotten a degree in journalism instead of marketing. Or, maybe I could have been an engineer or a doctor or something. But I don't know if that would have improved my quality of life, other than the satisfaction that I didn't waste four years of school.

"But I could have done a lot more. Everybody can. They ought to wait until they are about twenty-six years old before they go to college," Jimmy concludes.

Does Jimmy feel he's been successful?

"Well, what's success? I'll tell you what success is for me. I'm happy. I'm content with what I'm doing. I'm content with the amount of money I make. I'm content with what I save. Not to say I don't want any more, but that's not a pressing thing. I enjoy things, like working in the yard, even by myself.

"And my wife likes to work in the yard, too. She's a contractor and she stays busy most of the time. I tell her, 'you ought to quit.' But she's the same way I am. She enjoys being a contractor, and it has the perk to it that it does make money. But she would probably do it if she was breaking even because she enjoys doing that," Jimmy adds.

Meanwhile, Wade, who has authored numerous scientific papers and publications, is a sought-after authority in his field. He is one of the first four surgeons in the United States, and the first in the South, to perform the new procedure that combines glaucoma and cataract surgery. He taught a course on the subject at the Academy of Ophthalmology in Orlando and also flew to Chicago to present a paper on the matter. At the time, he had performed more of the procedures than anybody else in the country.

Faulkner has lived to see both his sons achieve financial success.

"Wade started making good money right off, and they had three kids, but I don't think he reached the millionaire stage until he was about thirty-two or thirty-three. He used to inform me how much he made, but he doesn't inform me now. I don't think he even knows. I just know he spends a lot, more than he should, probably.

"But anyway, I kind of lectured him about it the other day. He said he felt he was doing his part taking care of the children. I said, 'Maybe you are not being fair to them. Have you ever thought of that? Maybe they want to make it their own way.'

"But Jimmy's children are not too well off financially, and in fact some of them fuss about it. Jimmy sort of lets them bore with their own augers, but they are doing all right. But I doubt that any of them has their own home paid for," Faulkner said.

Wade said he does not resent the time nor money his father has devoted to the church.

"I think it's fine. Have I ever been envious of thinking that that was my inheritance? Never! I understand. I just never questioned it. It just seems like that's always been the case.

"Even when I thought that a twenty-dollar bill was a big piece of money, I remember that he would put a roll of them in the collection plate. I don't know where his desire to give came from, probably his mother, who I never knew. I haven't been told that, but that's what I think. A lot of it came through her. She must have been quite a woman.

Don't try to be an earthly saint,
with eyes fixed on a star,
Just try to be the fellow that
your mother thinks you are.
Will S. Adkin

Whatever differences the two sons may have, they were united in the love of their mother. Evelyn Faulkner provided the warmth, the nurturing, guidance, and love as the constant caretaker of her boys. An accomplished pianist, she often filled the home with music to accompany her good humor and energy.

"The best description, I think, is what a sweet and loving person she was," remembers Wade.

"People that I see as patients who knew her forever, always mention how sweet she was. That is what they always say. What a sweet, pretty woman she was."

Jimmy agrees.

"I have a lot of pleasant memories of her. She saw me through everything ... the Cub Scouts, the Scouts, and playing in the band."

Jimmy also remembers how she playfully avoided revealing her true age.

"I never did know exactly how old she was until after I was married because she always fibbed to us about her age. She was older than Daddy."

Wade is not sure how she was able to keep her age a secret for so long.

"How would I know? I never questioned it. It was just confusing to me. She always told me she was a year younger than Daddy, and she wasn't. But she never told me that until she turned eighty. So I was always confused about her age," Wade smiles.

Evelyn especially treasured the vacations and trips she shared with her husband and traveling companions. They would take from two to three trips each year, and Evelyn enjoyed visiting areas she had never seen before. But at least once a year they would head for Hot Springs, Arkansas, to luxuriate in the hot mineral waters, take side trips to the nearby countryside, and share dinner with close friends. This was a practice she relished as long as her health would permit.

Finally, illness overtook this wife and mother of the Faulkner clan, and it was a difficult experience for the entire family, especially her husband.

"During our married life, she had to have nineteen major operations and suffered constantly during the last four years while practically an invalid. She had to have nurses with her around the clock. Knowing that she was not going to ever be able to recover, I was able to accustom myself to the fact that she would not be with me much longer. But of course, you are never ready for it when the time comes. It is not easy to lose a loved one, especially a wife with whom you have lived for almost fifty-nine years.

"The children had also become accustomed to the idea of her dying, even though they loved her very much. They were comforted with the fact that they had been able to know her since their birth. This included the two sons, as well as the grandchildren. We did not do a lot of talking about her death but understood each other in our sadness, and more or less adjusted ourselves to the fact," Faulkner stated.

Wade especially remembered the last year of her illness.

"It was a long, drawn out thing. She just got weaker and weaker and lost more and more weight. She was in a lot of pain, and she was on a lot of pain medication then. She was not very lucid, there was not a lot of communication. It was not a very pleasant thing, but she had been sick for a long time."

Jimmy Junior remembered the night she died.

"They called me and I knew something had happened. It was something like 2 or 3 in the morning and they said, 'Your mother has died.'

"I went over there and I looked, and I asked the nurse, 'Are you sure?' And the nurse said, 'I've never been wrong before.' So I called the funeral home.

"It was sad, in a way, but it wasn't crying sad because we knew she was going to die. She had lost a lot of weight and she couldn't take care of herself.

"I don't know exactly how old she was when she died, but she must have been close to eighty, because she was older than Daddy. I don't know how much, maybe two or three years, because she always lied about her age," Jimmy smiled.

Evelyn Irwin Faulkner, a life-long resident of Bay Minette, died in her home on Monday, October 30, 1995. She was eighty-five. The funeral, one of the largest the city has ever known, was held from the Bay Minette church of Christ and she was laid to rest in Bay Minette Cemetery, less than a mile east of her home.

"She had designated certain of her personal belongings to each of the grandchildren and it was a pleasure to present them with the jewelry and other items that she wanted them to have, of which she had made a list before dying," Faulkner concluded.

I grew up in a strict family. My dad thought you would go straight to hell if you danced or played cards.

Karlene Faulkner

10

Dearest Friends

When Jimmy Faulkner was a barefoot youth trodding the clay hills of Lamar County, he could only dream of far away places and read about cities like Paris and London. As a youth, he would attend school in New Mexico, college in Tennessee and a university in Missouri. But as an adult, travel would become a major part of his life and he would venture throughout the country and around the world and take advantage of nearly every opportunity to see new places and meet new people.

His career itinerary has taken him to ninety-one foreign countries and his goal is to visit one hundred before he reaches the age of one hundred. Sometimes his trips are for business, seeking new industries to locate in his community. Other times, he travels with friends simply for pleasure.

On a trip to Paris, Faulkner remembers the morning he left his room in the hotel to have breakfast in the downstairs restaurant. He ordered a half cantaloupe and couldn't believe the price of $9.50. He remembered as a youth that the family had cantaloupes that the worms would eat before they could get them out of the field. Now, he was paying nearly ten dollars for just a half a cantaloupe.

Two of the Faulkners' dearest traveling companions were M. C. and Karlene Farmer. The Farmers owned a construction company in nearby Mobile. When Faulkner decided to run for governor, M. C. was a supporter and helped raise money for Faulkner in both races, 1954 and 1958.

"He had a lot of friends over the state and he raised money for me. He was very active in my campaign," Faulkner remembers.

Their friendship continued to grow through their business contacts, their political support of George Wallace for governor, and their travels. Both men were pilots, which was an added convenience in their frequent trips. Farmer would usually serve as pilot because he owned the airplane. Faulkner would be co-pilot and navigator.

While the men had traveled together on business numerous times, the first overseas trip for the two couples was to Spain and Portugal. It was a very enjoyable trip and marked the beginning of a long travel relationship. For some thirty or more years the Faulkners and Farmers would enjoy their trips together.

"We traveled together nearly all over the world and all over the United States and we got along fine," Faulkner remembers. "When we would plan a trip, M. C. would say, 'Well, you just plan it and if I don't like it I'll fuss at you,'" Faulkner laughs.

"M. C. didn't believe much in history. He had this saying, 'let bygones be bygones.' One time we were driving from Salt Lake City to Yellowstone, and we passed this sign that said 'Golden Spike,' with an arrow pointing the direction. The site was about twenty miles out of our way and I knew M. C. would not be interested, so I just quietly drove to see the Golden Spike. It was a good attraction with a ceremony showing the history of how the railroads were joined at this location. But until he died, M. C. fussed at me for driving twenty miles out of the way to see the Golden Spike. He just didn't care for geography or history. And when we were traveling, he was dead set against retreating or going out of the way.

"When we were in Sundance, Wyoming, we saw a picture on the wall of this little restaurant depicting 'Devil's Rock,' which was featured in a movie. It was about fifteen miles from where we had turned off the main road. We were on our way to see Mount Rushmore and the carvings of the presidents. The rest of us wanted to go back and see Devil's Rock, so we told M. C. a little fib. He asked us if we were retreating, and I told him that this was the shortest way to where we are going. Of course, when we got there M. C. was not interested in the rock, but they also had a city of prairie dogs there and he was really interested in those prairie dogs.

"I remember once we were in Cairo and we were going to an Egyptian museum. We had to climb a large number of steps to get to the top. M. C. didn't want to go up there, but we started out. By the time we got halfway up the steps, M. C. turned to my wife and said, 'Evelyn, if there are two chairs up there when we get to the top, you can have one of them,'" Faulkner laughed.

Faulkner described Farmer as "a very close friend" who did not have much formal education but was a very smart, successful businessman.

"He had a great amount of common sense. I have never seen anybody who could identify a problem, analyze it, and determine the solution just like that! He was a brilliant man, and very frugal," Faulkner recalls.

While both men were excellent pilots, neither had a current instrument rating. Faulkner had worked with instruments in the military but felt he should acquire the instrument rating. The two men decided to go out to Fort Worth, Texas, and take the instrument rating course.

"He knew a lot more about it than I did. He taught me more at night than I learned in the daytime in the school," Faulkner added.

When the two finally took the test, both passed, and received their ratings.

Farmer's interest in aviation led to his appointment by the mayor of Mobile to the city's Airport Authority. He served as chairman of the authority for a number of years and was the driving force in the construction of the new airport terminal in Mobile. The city dedicated the new terminal for Farmer and placed a bronze bust of him in front of it.

The Faulkners and the Farmers remained dear friends for years, often spending special occasions together. In fact, in 1986 the two couples had made plans to have Christmas dinner together. Early Christmas morning, Faulkner received a telephone call from his close friend Matthew Metcalfe, a next-door neighbor of the Farmers, who told Faulkner, "Jimmy, we've lost M. C."

Faulkner was shocked. He knew that M. C. had experienced some difficulty with his heart, but did not realize it was so serious. The entire city paid tribute to their beloved friend but no one felt the pain more sharply than the Faulkners.

KARLENE

For more than fifty-one years M. C. and Karlene Farmer had been more than husband and wife. They had been dear friends, close companions in life, and partners in the business they operated together. His sudden death was unexpected.

"It was a shock. I knew from his activities that he had not been feeling well, that something was wrong. Still, the doctors had conducted tests and couldn't find the problem. He had experienced difficulty flying because of the pressure, but the doctors didn't know what it was or where it was coming from. He had gone back for checkups and examinations, but they found nothing,"

Karlene said. Reluctantly she agreed to the doctors' request for an autopsy. The aneurysm was behind his heart, and would have been inoperable.

News of Farmer's death was on the radio Christmas morning. He was well-known in Mobile, and the recent publicity of the dedication of the airport terminal in his honor was fresh in the minds of the people. Farmer also was a leader in Dauphin Way Baptist Church and was named chairman of the fund-raising committee for the new building program a month before he died.

"The night that he died, we held a vespers service at the funeral home on a site that overlooked the new church construction. We could see some of the steel coming up out of the ground, and I thought how he would have loved to have lived to see it completed," Karlene remembered. "It's a beautiful church now and it thrills me to see it, because M. C. was so interested in it."

The church family and the pastor were particularly helpful to Karlene in providing support and comfort during this difficult time. Of special assistance was Ahledia Seever, widow of a Baptist minister, who was Karlene's dearest friend and a bedrock of support for more than a decade after the loss.

"Sometimes you just have to find the inner strength to carry on. I guess it was some months later before I really took the time to grieve, which is not good. You need to go ahead and grieve when it happens, but I couldn't do that," she noted.

What does Karlene remember most about M. C.?

"His loving nature. His love for people, and the fact that he really loved me. I know he did. We had a very compatible, happy marriage."

Karlene credits her faith in God and her dear friends for helping her cope with the loss of her husband. She has been a Christian since she was twelve years old.

A product of the depression years, Annie Karlene Frazier was born November 23, 1913, in Johnson County, Georgia. She was the eldest of six children, and the only girl. For twelve years her family lived far out in the country, and she walked three miles to and from school every day. Later, her parents bought a house in Adrian, a small country town in Georgia located halfway between Macon and Savannah on Highway 80. It was here that she finished high school.

"I don't recall too much about my childhood. I came from a happy home, a Christian home. My father in later years became disabled because of glaucoma, which runs in the family, and he became blind.

"I grew up in a strict family. My dad thought you would go straight to hell if you danced or played cards. We had some neighbors who were very good to us. They did a lot of different things, and they would take us to picture shows occasionally. But we made our own fun. We youngsters would meet at the post office on Sunday afternoons and went for a walk along the railroad track to the river, which was about three miles. And, of course, we would go to church," Karlene remembers.

It was during the depression years when Karlene graduated from high school that a young man named Mathew Carlton Farmer came to Adrian on a construction job. He was working on a crew to raise a bridge across the nearby Ohoopee River.

"While he was there, we courted. We dated and saw each other as much as we could, but dating in a small town back then was different from dating now. He would come by the house and we would go to church, and things like that. We just became friends, and as it happened, we found that we loved each other, and I went to meet his mother. His father had died when he was real young and he was devoted to his mother. Before he left to go to another job, we became engaged. Some months later, we were married in a private ceremony in the parsonage of a Baptist minister in Opelika, Alabama, in 1935.

"M. C. was in the construction field, so we did a lot of moving around. We moved to Athens, Alabama, where he worked for the Tennessee Valley Authority on various construction jobs, and then we went to the Gulf Coast where we lived for several years.

"When the war broke out, he had a job building military camps. We knew that M. C. could be called to go into service at any time, so we decided that I should take some kind of training to make a living. I went to Draughn's Business College in Little Rock. It was there that M. C. enlisted into the Civil Engineer Corps of the Navy in 1943. When he went to camp, I returned home for a short time until I could join him in Williamsburg, Virginia," she said.

Shortly after, M. C. was transferred to New York to receive training as a stevedore. Soon he received orders for overseas duty in New Guinea and the Philippines. Karlene, meanwhile, returned to Georgia for a short time until she was called to work by the company that had employed her husband. This marked the beginning of her career as a field office manager in the construction industry.

Following the war, the company, and the Farmers, transferred to Mobile to the company's new headquarters. The Farmers established their home in Mobile and M. C. worked with the firm for four years, preparing to go into business for himself.

M. C. Farmer Contracting, which later became Farmer Construction Company, was organized in 1950 and required the best efforts of both M. C. and Karlene. They worked together in the firm for years with Karlene operating the office and handling much of the finances while M. C. would bid and supervise the work projects.

"M. C. did not have a formal education to amount to anything.

I think he got to the seventh grade in school. However, he had a keen mind and a great sense of how to get along with people. It was uncanny how he could out-figure other estimators on jobs. They would work two or three days, while in minutes he could come up with round figures that would be almost exactly what they had estimated," Karlene remembered.

For years the Farmers, who had no children, would work side by side with little time for outside activities. But in 1951, Karlene joined the Pilot Club, a civic organization, and they both became members of the Dauphin Way Baptist Church.

"I was real active in the Pilot Club and went to conventions. Evelyn and Jimmy would join us for the trips. We would fly there, then we would rent a car, drive all over the area, like Canada, then fly back home," Karlene remembered.

Karlene served as president of her local club and also served as committee chair for conventions. She attended more than thirty conventions which provided her the opportunity to travel all over the United States. On the international level, she served on the Advisory Board of the Pilot International Foundation.

Meanwhile, M. C. served on the finance committee of their church and both were involved in raising funds for the new building. Karlene served as president of the Woman's Missionary Union and as program director for the "Together We Build" campaign to raise money to relocate the church. She also worked for thirty-five years in the Sunday School departments and served on search committees for the selection of two pastors.

The Farmers also became involved in Mobile College, a Baptist institution supported by their church. M. C. served as a trustee. Karlene was a founding member of the Mobile College Auxiliary and served as its first vice president, and co-chairman of the Scholarship Committee.

Mobile College is now known as the University of Mobile where an M. C. and Karlene Farmer Scholarship Fund has been established for students preparing for full-time Christian service. A building in honor of M. C. Farmer, which bears his name, was dedicated in 1998. Karlene served as a trustee of the college from 1985 to 1995 and also serves on the Foundation Board.

Karlene became involved in numerous civic activities including the fine arts, the opera, senior citizens organizations, education, Goodwill industries, and the Mobile Historic Society. In 1988 Karlene received the distinguished honor of being named First Lady of Mobile and was given a Scroll of Merit. The honoree is chosen by the citizens of Mobile from among those nominated for distinguished service in a worthy field. Karlene was nominated and selected for her work in her church. And in 1991, Karlene was given an honorary Doctor of Letters degree by Mobile College.

Second Romance

Years passed after the death of M. C. as Karlene, with the help of her almost inseparable companion, Ahledia Seever, struggled to return some form of normalcy to her life. However, she had no idea in her mind of marrying again. In fact, she would go out of her way to avoid even the appearance of any romantic interests.

Finally, on one occasion, Jimmy Faulkner, who had grieved for the loss of his own partner, invited Karlene and her friend Ahledia to meet for dinner at the Blue Gill, a quaint but modest seafood restaurant overlooking the bay between Mobile and Bay Minette.

"She was very aloof," remembers Faulkner. "Before I got there, Karlene had sat on one side of the table right in the middle, so I had to sit on the other side with her friend. She did that just to make sure no one could accuse her of dating," Faulkner smiles.

As time passed, Mr. and Mrs. Matthew (Matt) Metcalfe, mutual friends of both Jimmy and Karlene and next door neighbors of Karlene, planned a trip to Bermuda. Since both Jimmy and Karlene had long shared a love for travel with their companions, the Metcalfes insisted that the four make the trip to Bermuda.

"Of course we had separate rooms, and Karlene insisted on paying for herself. But I guess that it was on that trip that she began to relax somewhat and began to warm up a little," Faulkner recalls.

After the trip, Jimmy and Karlene would see each other, but mostly in the company of the Metcalfes.

"We'd go to dinner. And when he would be in town, he'd call me and take me to dinner. When he would come back from a trip, he would come by to see me," Karlene remembers.

Did Karlene think about marriage?

"It was the furthest thing from my mind that I would ever get married again. I thought that I had done my dues with fifty-one and a half years of happy marriage.

"But Jimmy and I enjoyed each other and the first thing I knew, it got serious. I had to spend a lot of time down on my knees praying, trying to work it out. Like I say, marriage was the furthermost thing in my mind."

Months went by, and Jimmy proposed to Karlene at her home. On June 22, 1996, the two were married in a private ceremony.

"We got married at Wade's home in Daphne. They have a lovely home there on a bluff overlooking Mobile Bay, and they had a reception for the immediate family members and a few very close friends. It was real sweet, and Wade and Ann had everything looking so pretty. I had asked Dr. Darrel Robinson, who had been my pastor but had moved to Atlanta, to conduct the wedding for us," Karlene recalls.

Faulkner had bought a new suit for the occasion and Wade's wife, Ann, had taken Karlene to an exclusive dress shop in Pensacola to select a wedding dress. "It was a beautiful dress, and she still won't tell me how much it cost," Faulkner laughs.

Karlene is especially grateful that she has been so warmly received by Faulkner's two sons, and the entire Faulkner family. Son Wade was quick to compliment his stepmother.

"I could tell you volumes about her. Let me put it this way, my Dad is mighty lucky to have her. She's a fine, wonderful person and we all like her. Daddy got me and Jimmy together for dinner one day in Bay Minette and he said he wanted to have a serious conversation. Jimmy and I looked at each other and suddenly both of us knew exactly what he was talking about. We said, 'Go ahead and marry Karlene!'

"We both are crazy about her, and we can't say enough about what a fine woman she is. The church she attended in Mobile is just down the street from my office and the members of the congregation who are my patients still tell me how much they hated to lose her to Bay Minette, and they say wonderful things about her."

The newlyweds invited the Metcalfes to join them for their honeymoon trip, a cruise down the coast of California to Mexico, with a few days at Laguna Beach.

Prior to leaving on the honeymoon, the newlyweds had begun renovation of the back portion of the Faulkner home to include a bright sunroom overlooking the back yard, and kitchen improvements. The construction was to be completed before their return.

"The night we came back from our honeymoon, the kitchen was ripped out, the refrigerator was sitting in the middle of the floor, the furniture was in the bathroom and the room was being painted. Jimmy was so upset. I said, 'Oh, that's all right,' and I cleared off the bed in the back bedroom," Karlene remembers.

Does Faulkner believe his wife has adjusted to living in the smaller town of Bay Minette?

"Yes, I would say so. She misses her friends in Mobile, of course, but it's only about thirty miles away and she drives herself once or twice a week to take care of her business and to see some of her friends. But it has been a major change for her. The most drastic change, I believe, has been the church. She attended a church that had a thousand or more in Sunday School, where here, we may have perhaps seventy-five. But her dear friend, Ahledia, who helped her so much and was in charge of our wedding arrangements and the flowers, died within a month after our wedding. She was Karlene's main contact in Mobile. Losing her friend may have made it a little easier to live in Bay Minette as Karlene would have been pretty much by herself in Mobile."

The sale of the construction company and disposition of the firm's equipment left Karlene financially independent, and she now manages her investments and makes her own financial decisions. She believes that it is helpful to the relationship that both partners are financially independent.

"That has a lot to do with it. I think that helps a lot. I feel independent. I have the resources to do what I want to do," she says.

Karlene did not cut all her ties to Mobile. In fact, she kept her home which she still maintains.

"It gives us a place so that when he goes out of Mobile on an early flight, he can spend the night there. Or if he's in town, and he has time between appointments and needs to rest, he has a place. I have a maid that goes by four days a week," she said.

Were there any major surprises in the marriage for her?

"I knew him pretty well. There were no big surprises. I was pretty sure there wouldn't be. That's the advantage in marrying someone who has been your friend, and who you have known under all circumstances."

Does she have any major concerns now?

"The only thing I worry about is that every day that goes by, I am less likely to be independent. But I don't have any particular worry. I worry about his health a little, but that's natural for me to do that. I'm a worrier, and he's an optimist. That's one of the things about him that I enjoy very much. He never looks on the dark side. When he has a problem, he manages to come up with the solution. If he can't solve it one way, he'll come at it from another direction. He's like a bulldog, he never turns loose," Karlene affirms.

Karlene says she likes to spend her time now meeting her husband's needs and keeping him happy.

"We go to dinner, take friends to dinner, and are invited out to dinner a lot. I guess that's the main thing. It doesn't take a lot to make me happy," she said.

She feels her purpose in life is "to be of service to others, and to be a good wife to the most active octogenarian I have ever known."

My slogan was "Honesty, Progress and Decency." For some reason, the word decency was not too popular as many thought I was a little too decent and straight to be governor.

Jimmy Faulkner

Jimmy Faulkner's parents: Henry L. and Ebbie Johnson Faulkner. Mrs. Faulkner, pictured below with her parents and siblings, was one of fourteen children.

Henry Faulkner built this farmhouse for his family in the Star community near Vernon, Alabama. He died in a fire in the house in 1928 when Jimmy was twelve years old.

Jimmy Faulkner's childhood companion was his older brother, Thurston, who grew up to become an educator.

After he moved to Bay Minette to become a newspaper publisher, Jimmy met Evelyn Irwin. They were married from 1937 until her death in 1995. (These photos were made in the 1950s.)

When World War II came, Faulkner served first as the deputy director of Alabama's War Bonds effort. In 1943, he enlisted in the Army Air Corps and after his own pilot training was made a flight instructor in multi-engine bombers.

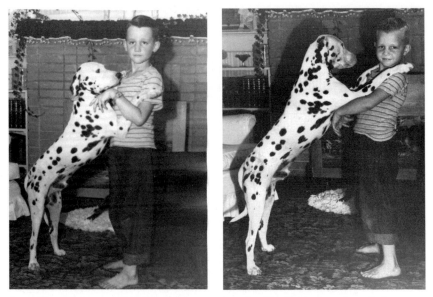

Sons Jimmy Jr. and Wade Faulkner, with the family Dalmatian. Below, a later photo with Jimmy Jr., Evelyn, Wade, and Jimmy Faulkner.

In 1954, Faulkner made the first of his two campaigns for the Democratic nomination for governor of Alabama.

As a newspaper publisher and broadcast executive, Faulkner understood earlier than many politicans the effective use of media and polling. One of his trademarks was a statewide "talkathon."

Faulkner's long service in state government brought him into a close relationship with Governor George C. Wallace. Above, Wallace listens as Faulkner speaks in the state senate on behalf of a Wallace measure. Presiding in the background is Robert Vance, later a federal judge who was killed by a mail bomb. Below, Faulkner with James Blackwood, of the famous Blackwood Brothers Quartet gospel group; Lurleen Wallace; Louisiana's "Singing Governor" Jimmie Davis, who wrote and recorded "You Are My Sunshine"; and Wallace.

Faulkner also enjoyed a close friendship with U.S. Senator James B. "Jim" Allen. Left, Faulkner and Allen pose with Faulkner's great-uncle Burrell on the occasion of his 100th birthday in April 1969.

Below, Faulkner in 1992 with Jimmy Clarke, Speaker of the House, and Jamelle Folsom, widow of one governor and mother of another.

Even after he was out of politics, Faulkner continued to work with Alabama governors on projects involving industry and education. Above, he and Evelyn visit with Governor and Mrs. Guy Hunt at the Governor's Mansion in 1987. Below, he confers with Governor Fob James at the 1998 dedication of the Visionland theme park in Birmingham.

Above, Faulkner with retired U.S. Senator Howell Heflin (center), and Matthew Metcalfe, longtime friend and travel companion and former business partner.

Below, Jimmy and Karlene Faulkner with U.S.M.C. Maj. Gen. Gary Cooper (left) and U.S. Secretary of State Colin Powell, 1995.

In 1974, Faulkner and son Jimmy Jr. (standing, right) sold their newspaper holdings to Frank Helderman, Jr. (seated, right) and his newspaper chain. Also pictured is Lamar Benton of the Helderman group.

Since 1958, Faulkner has worked with Volkert & Associates. Here he is with CEO Keith King, on the site of a long-term client, the Alabama State Docks. Behind them is an award-winning Volkert project, the Cochrane/ Africatown USA bridge in north Mobile.

Faulkner representing Volkert & Associates at a meeting in the Palace of the Amir of Bahrain, with H. H. Prince Mohammed al Sulman al Khalifa.

Jimmy and Evelyn Faulkner, with University of North Alabama President Dr. Bob Guillot, on the occasion of Faulkner receiving an honorary doctor of laws degree from the university, December 1984.

Dorothy Martin, Faulkner's executive assistant for more than a half century.

George Noonan of the North Baldwin Chamber of Commerce presents Faulkner with one of his most unusual awards: the "Man of the Century" designated by the people of Bay Minette and Baldwin County for the person who had done the most for the county in the twentieth century.

Above, the Faulkner home on Fifth Street in Bay Minette, in 1973 after a rare south Alabama snowfall. Left, Alvina and April Shi, Faulkner's "adopted" Chinese "grandchildren." Below, a 1970s family outing on a Mississippi riverboat.

Above, Faulkner with sons Jimmy Jr., left, and Wade, on the occasion of his 1996 marriage to Karlene Farmer.

Left, Jimmy and Karlene Faulkner, Christmas 2000.

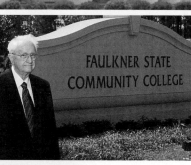

Top, at Faulkner
University; inset, at
Faulkner State
Community College.

Left, Jimmy and
Karlene Faulkner
with former
Montgomery Mayor
Emory Folmar, at the
1996 dedication of
Faulkner University's
Jones School of Law.

The Faulkner family, Christmas 2001, at the Faulkner home in Bay Minette (from left): Molly Harris, Mary Jane Harris, Daniel Harris, Floyd Harris, Jenny Camp, Claire Camp, Caroline Camp, Andrew Camp, Jimmy Faulkner Jr., Allen Todd, Beverly Faulkner, Rachel Todd, Steve Todd, Jane Anne Stewart, Andy Stewart, Louise Stewart, Rebecca Stewart, Will Faulkner, Rascal, Jim Faulkner III, Sol Faulkner, Karlene Faulkner, Jimmy Faulkner, Wade Faulkner, Ann Faulkner, Francis Taupeka, Jay Faulkner, Paul Michael Taupeka, Beth Taupeka, Paul Taupeka, Wade Faulkner Jr.

11

The World of Politics

B arely in his twenties, Faulkner served as co-county campaign manager for the candidacy of Frank Dixon in the 1938 governor's race. His own first venture for political office was for mayor of Bay Minette in 1940.

"I was twenty-four and had no thought of getting into a political race. A group approached me about running for city council and I immediately told them I was not interested.

"Then, I was approached by the current mayor, aging J. C. Burns, who did not want to run again, and asked me if I would run. Considering his age, experience, business success, and the fact that he was just an all-around fine citizen, I was flattered by his request and got to thinking about it," Faulkner remembers.

Meanwhile, a group of ladies from the town led by Mrs. R. V. Vail, whose husband had sold him the *Baldwin Times,* approached Faulkner about running for mayor. They learned that he had some interest in the job, but he gave the women no commitment that he would run. The small group got busy collecting signatures on petitions until they had gathered enough to assure victory. At this point, Faulkner agreed to become a candidate.

Faulkner overwhelmingly defeated his one opponent, city coun-
cilman John Beebe, a local attorney, and was soon dubbed "The
Youngest Mayor in America." He served the city until he volunteered for the Army Air Corps in 1943. He was succeeded by L. D.
Owen, Sr.

Before entering military service, Faulkner also served as co-
campaign chairman for Baldwin County for Chauncey Sparks in
the 1942 governor's race.

"Sparks, like Frank Dixon, was elected and here I was still a
youngster and had been successful in helping to elect two governors, which was encouraging on my part," Faulkner recalls.

"Sparks had been considered un-electable because everyone in
the state seemed to be for two-time governor Bibb Graves, who was
thought to have the election in the bag, when he died. Chris
Sherlock, who had been Graves's highway director and friend, had
announced his candidacy before Graves's death, stating that he was
standing by in case something happened to Graves. However,
Graves's followers resented this and went almost entirely to the
Sparks camp. I had previously agreed to be Graves's campaign
manager, but instead worked for Sparks in the same capacity,"
Faulkner noted.

After Sparks won, he offered Faulkner a job as assistant to the
Speaker of the House of Representatives in Montgomery, but the
young newspaper publisher turned it down, having married and
begun a family and having already acquired an enormous debt for
a youngster still in the depression days.

Faulkner then spent three years in the Air Corps, becoming a
bomber pilot and pilot instructor.

Alabama State Senator

In the summer of 1945, Faulkner returned to Bay Minette from his military service. He resumed editing and publishing the *Baldwin Times.*

Money was tight after the war, and soldiers returning home needed a place to live. Faulkner was determined to see what could be done to arrange financing to build new houses. He was success-ful in his effort and received financing for about twenty homes. Although he found this success rewarding, he soon realized that he had to decide whether he would be a house builder or a publisher. He returned his attention to his first love, his newspaper.

Soon, he was approached by a large delegation urging him to run for Probate Judge.

"This did not interest me. But I did get to thinking about running for the state senate. Just when and why I thought about this, I do not know, but it was prior to 1948.

"In 1948, after having been elected to the State Democratic Executive Committee from the Second Congressional District, which included Bay Minette to Montgomery, I was asked to run for delegate to the Democratic National Convention from the district. There were six in the race, but Jeff Beeland of Greenville and I were the victors. I ran second as Beeland was a well-known name and mine was not, at the time.

"This was the famous 1948 convention in Philadelphia, in which Harry Truman was nominated and the Dixiecrat Party was formed in reaction to Truman's famous speech declaring the end of segregation in American schools," Faulkner noted.

Unknown at that time to these Alabama delegates, the event would set into motion a civil rights movement, spurred later by the *Brown v. Board of Education* U.S. Supreme Court decision, that would change the face of Alabama politics for years. Race would rise as a dominant political issue in campaigns yet to come.

"George Wallace rode to the convention with Evelyn and me,

along with Roy Noland, Jr., postmaster of Montgomery. There were twenty-six delegates to the convention, and we were among the thirteen who did not walk out. The other thirteen did and became the nucleus of the Dixiecrat Party in Alabama, which was really headed by former governor Frank Dixon.

"While we were in Philadelphia, B. B. Larrimore of Robertsdale, who had attended as an onlooker, told me he was going to run for mayor of Robertsdale, and then run for the state senate. His father-in-law was a member of the legislature from Chilton County. Larrimore ran for mayor and got sixteen votes and apparently never thought of the senate any more. But when he told me his plan in Philadelphia, I thought to myself that I was going to run for this office, too. And I did," Faulkner remembered.

At the time, this senate district included Baldwin, Monroe, and Escambia counties. There existed a "gentlemen's agreement" that the senate position would be switched every four years, giving each county an opportunity to furnish a senator every twelve years. The prospect of serving in the Alabama Senate intrigued Faulkner.

"I had three opponents. One was a local attorney, C. Lenoir Thompson, who had been to Washington as the administrative assistant to Robin Swift, who had been appointed U.S. Senator when John Bankhead died. Thompson had intended to run for the state senate for a long time and had a lot of friends in the area.

"Another opponent was Jim Carney, Sr., who lived in Daphne and was a renowned citizen, having Carney Station on the L&N Railroad, just east of Bay Minette, named for his family. He was a fine, old gentleman.

"And much to my surprise, Frank Earle also decided to run. It was surprising because Earle had come to my office and asked me to run, saying the county did not need W. C. (Buddy) Holmes as senator. I discovered that Earle was encouraged to run when a small group of Bay Minette citizens met for dinner one night in George Stevenson's home. They decided to get Frank Earle to run for the senate because he was bound to win. He was chairman of the Baldwin County Board of Education, president of the Baldwin County Farm Bureau, chairman of the REA Board, and a long-time outstanding citizen who had worked closely with the farmers and others in the county.

"He and I had been friends since I arrived in the county in 1936, and his announcement against me was disappointing, although not disturbing," Faulkner said.

The senatorial district was the biggest in geographic area in the state and Faulkner worked day and night in the campaign. There were political rallies in Escambia and Baldwin counties, but none in Monroe. All that was needed in Monroe was the support of the popular probate judge. When schedules conflicted, Faulkner would dispatch his newspaper editor, Bob Morrissette, to fill in for him. At other times, one of his two sons, who were nine and twelve, would substitute for the candidate.

"At the time, Judge E. T. (Shorty) Millsap was probate judge of Monroe County. Afterwards, many people in Montgomery asked me if Judge Millsap supported me. My answer was always, 'I carried Monroe County.' They smiled, knowing that he did. And in several boxes, I got every vote that was cast," Faulkner adds.

"Fortunately, I was elected with fifty-one percent of the vote, thus eliminating a runoff. Thompson ran second, Earle third, and Carney fourth. All the candidates congratulated me except my old friend, Earle.

"I was the first Baldwin County state senator to be elected in forty-eight years whose name was not 'Holmes.' Dr. Sibley Holmes had served one or two terms and then, prior to my election, Dr. Buddy Holmes was our senator," Faulkner smiles.

In the same election, James B. Allen became Lieutenant Governor of Alabama, and thus the presiding officer of the state senate. Allen, who later became a United States Senator, appointed Faulkner chairman of the education committee.

"This gave me the opportunity of introducing what turned out to be the finest retirement system for teachers and other state employees in the United States. The bill I sponsored made Alabama the first state in the nation to also include Social Security with the regular state retirement. Today, when a person is old enough to retire and old enough to draw Social Security, the take-home pay can be more than when the person was working. Our system is recognized everywhere as the best retirement in the U.S.," Faulkner boasts.

One of the greatest things he accomplished for his own county while serving in the state senate was to get the state to take over the county's road-building program. Faulkner says that according to the Auburn University Engineering Department, it became one of the finest road systems in Alabama and possibly in the United States. He explained how it all came about.

"E. N. Rodgers, former Baldwin County Highway Engineer and State Highway Director, told me that the state would like to have one county in Alabama to prove how efficient road building could be. He told me about it because we were good friends and because I was a state senator from Baldwin, Escambia, and Monroe counties at the time. Studying the subject further and learning that the states of Texas and Virginia had similar programs also, which were very successful, Representative L. W. Brannan and I proposed the legislation on a two-year trial basis, agreeing to leave it up to the county commissioners whether or not to extend it. Prior to that time, Baldwin County had only forty-one miles of paved, farm-to-market roads.

"The Baldwin County Commission was dubious at the time and one day Brannan called me from Montgomery and told me there was too much opposition and he was backing out unless I could change the attitude of some of the people. I then spoke to the Robertsdale Rotary Club and explained the situation to them. In spite of one of the county's commissioners who had said he was bitterly opposed to it, and others, at the end of my talk and after answering questions, the club, at that county commissioner's suggestion, voted unanimously to try out the system.

"The agreement was made with the county commission that we would put it on a trial basis for two years and, if they were not in favor of it at the end of this time, we would not continue it.

"The legislative measure itself turned all road building and maintenance over to the state. In turn, Baldwin County was to turn all of its road revenues over to the state.

"The state paved eighty-one miles in the next eighteen months, thus making this legislation very popular."

"In addition, in writing the bill, I quietly withheld from the legislation the automobile and truck tax license money and the two-and-a-half mill road and bridge funds from the state. That gave the county additional funds for the general fund, which was only getting three mills, where all other counties in Alabama were getting five. The county was able to get out of debt and the program proved very successful for twenty-eight years.

"At the end of the two-year period, the county commission voted unanimously to continue the system, which Brannan and I did. The state worked out a deal with the county where the state would furnish all the equipment needed on a rental basis and the county funds would only be used to pay for the equipment when actually in use. This saved untold amounts of money, too.

"The county also sold the state the equipment they had and

this, along with other savings, put the county completely out of debt for the first time in years, and kept it out of debt for a quarter of a century.

"One reason for the success of the state-run road system was P. B. (Buck) Day, who was put in charge of the county operation. Day was a hard-working, intelligent highway engineer who knew how to get work done efficiently and economically.

"First, he replaced hundreds of wooden bridges to improve the drainage of roads, which was causing so much damage. He built and paved roads at 60 percent of the cost under county operation.

"Six or seven other counties followed suit in Alabama, but their system was not as good as ours. Brannan and I put into our program that the county commissioners would continue to select the roads to be built since we figured the people did not elect us for this purpose. The other counties' legislators took charge of the road building and it led to considerable dissatisfaction.

"Unfortunately, when Fob James became governor, he listened to his highway director, Rex Rainer, and decided to abolish our system. This was one of the worst things that ever happened to Baldwin County.

"Rainer, who was dean of the engineering school at Auburn before his appointment to highway director, at one time had a crew make a study of Baldwin's road system and declared it to be the best in the state, the southeast, and possibly the nation. Yet, as highway director, he abolished it. For unknown reasons, he decided that the state should get out of Baldwin County and so recommended to Governor James, who took his word for it and agreed.

"After twenty-eight years of successful road building, the system was turned back over to the county and, as a result, millions of dollars of debt has piled up trying to keep up with the fast-growing population in need of roads. Now, we have duplication of road building facilities in the county, a lot of additional expenses and machinery. As you might expect, the county commissioners like it this way and the possibility of ever changing back to the more efficient system is not likely.

"Incidentally, the state of Virginia has one road system. The state highway department is in charge of all roads, state, county, and city. Thus, millions of dollars are saved because of the efficiency and economy.

"Before the change was made back to the county, I went to see Governor James and explained the situation to him. He was interested but simply said, 'Jimmy, I wish you had come to me earlier. It's too late now.' It wasn't too late, but Rex Rainer had sold him a bill of goods and sold Baldwin County down the road," Faulkner regrets.

Faulkner found that serving as a state senator provided him an excellent insight into state governmental affairs. Soon, the lieutenant governor, with the approval of Governor Gordon Persons, appointed him to serve on an interim finance and taxation committee. The committee was to meet before the first regular session of the legislature to decide what had to be done to get more money for education. The committee recommended the passage of the second one-cent sales tax for schools. The measure found little opposition from the people of the state.

"Another interesting assignment was made by the president pro-tem of the senate, Albert Boutwell of Jefferson County, who named me and Jimmy Morgan of Birmingham to a committee to make a special study and recommendations concerning the Alabama Medical School in Birmingham. The school was not very old, but obviously had great possibilities. Because of the lack of funds, they had not been able to accomplish very much. I recall that the previous year's appropriation was about $640,000 from the state.

Morgan and I recommended an appropriation of $1,013,000, which met with the governor's approval and was passed by the legislature. The people at the medical school have been my friends ever since, and it has been a pleasure knowing them."

Because of his position and his relationship with the governor, Faulkner was able to get several other things accomplished for his city and for Baldwin County.

"During this time, the Fish River Bridge was built on Highway 98. Up to that time the only way you could get across the river was by a ferry. This beautiful bridge was built for $150,000. It soon will be replaced with a four-lane bridge which will cost several million," Faulkner said.

Also, when Faulkner was in the state senate and Brannan was in the house of representatives, the two introduced a bill that would change forever the beautiful Gulf shoreline of Baldwin County.

"The bill we introduced would change the Alabama/Florida state line from the Perdido Pass Bridge to where it is today, about two miles east, between Old River and the Gulf.

"Earl McGowan of Chatom, Alabama, who was state conservation director, got the idea and helped us accomplish this unprecedented feat of changing state lines. Our argument was that when the two state lines were placed, the original state line was where it is now, but a hurricane came and changed the route of Old River and made it go west to Perdido Pass. At the time, there was nothing there but sand and it was no trouble getting the Alabama legislature to approve the bill. The proud part was getting Florida to agree to it. They did, because the land was of no value at the time, or so they thought. Also, the U.S. Congress had to approve it before it became finalized," Faulkner said.

"Now, towering condominiums and other buildings are on this strip of land and, of course, the property is worth millions."

Faulkner also sponsored a bill to permit national banks to lend money on standing timber in Alabama. This previously could not be done.

"I worked hard and generally enjoyed it, even though it worked a hardship, being gone from my family and the newspaper so much. I alternated taking Jimmy and Wade to Montgomery with me, each serving his week as a senate page," Faulkner recalls.

Faulkner's hard work paid off. The Capitol Press Corps selected him Alabama's "Outstanding Freshman Senator."

Govenor's Race — 1954

At thirty-six, Jimmy Faulkner had never even dreamed of running for governor of Alabama. But in the fall of 1953, *Montgomery Advertiser* columnist Allen Rankin dropped by Faulkner's office, claiming he wanted to write an article for the *Readers Digest* or a New York magazine about the successes of the Hilliard Jenkins family, an African-American family in the nearby Belforest Community.

"He came to my office asking if I would guide him to where they lived. I told him that if he would wait a few minutes I would take him, which I did.

"Much to my surprise, when I opened the *Advertiser* the following Sunday, there was a full-blown column asking why Jimmy Faulkner wouldn't be the proper man to beat Jim Folsom? Then the following Sunday, he wrote a follow-up column. Then, Dick Hudson, Jr., publisher of the *Advertiser*, called me and urged me to run.

"Even though I was young and did not have any money or much experience, I agreed to make the race."

Race was not a dominant issue at this period in Alabama's history, although racial segregation was preferred by the Big Mule alliance that had dominated the legislature and state government for decades. These power brokers, who represented big business and large farm owners, were mainly interested in keeping taxes down, controlling labor unions, and providing bare minimum support for education and other functions of state government.

After making his decision to run, Faulkner spent his first few weeks visiting throughout the state asking questions and seeking advice from politicos. Former Governor Chauncey Sparks discouraged the young senator, saying he would be "just another candidate." Others would echo the sentiment.

In Tuscaloosa, Faulkner paid a visit on his old friend Marc Ray "Foots" Clement, who had headed the War Savings Bonds Campaign in Alabama and years earlier had convinced the young publisher to work as his assistant. Clement was a big supporter of Alabama's U.S. senators and considered by many to be the brains behind the campaigns of both Lister Hill and John Sparkman.

"Foots told me positively that unless I could come up with something special to attract attention, I would not have a chance of winning. He told me about Governor Francis Cherry of Arkansas who had just run a race by getting on radio throughout the state for long hours, answering questions asked him by the people.

"I went to Little Rock and talked with the governor's executive assistant and he explained the system and told me how I could get in touch with the people who ran their talkathon. I contacted them and they agreed to come to Alabama and help me.

"We would set up the talkathon on the ground floor of a building, like an automobile dealership, and I would sit in the middle of the room with a microphone and answer questions that were called in. The phone numbers were well advertised and people would call their questions in to my two helpers and they would write them down on a slip of paper and hand them over to me.

"The secret of it was being able to answer the questions. I had studied many hours learning the budgets of various state agencies and other details that were important to the voters. As a matter of fact, I might have been a little too smart in knowing the answers in the minds of some people. It doesn't hurt to be dumb every now and then," Faulkner smiles.

Faulkner believes he made a big mistake by starting the talkathon too early in the campaign.

"We had no money and Robert Luckie of Birmingham, a beginner in the advertising agency business who later became one of the biggest agencies in the state, agreed to handle my campaign. I owed him $30,000 and he was about to go under. This was eight weeks before voting time and everybody was urging me to get started with my talkathon.

"I knew it was too early. I wanted to start the talkathon four weeks out instead of eight, but we needed to get out and raise some money. I had three twenty-four hour talkathons, the first being in Montgomery, the second in Mobile, and the third in Birmingham.

"To say the very least, the Montgomery talkathon was tremendously successful and I began getting a lot of support. Grover C. Hall, the editorial writer of the *Montgomery Advertiser,* stated in an editorial that 'Jimmy Faulkner is headed to the State Capitol like a martin to his gourd.'

"I used the campaign to ask people to contribute 'Dollars for Decency.' My slogan was 'Honesty, Progress and Decency.' For some reason, the word decency was not too popular as many thought I was a little too decent and straight to be governor."

Faulkner's main opponent in the race, James E. "Big Jim" Folsom, had the full support of almost all county officials and political activists in the state.

"Sure enough, about ten days before voting time, I began to run out of money and lost the election, even though I was second."

Lieutenant Governor James B. Allen came in third in the seven-man race. Folsom won the race, escaping a runoff with Faulkner by only 7,385 votes out of a total of 596,001 votes cast.

"Amazingly, the whole campaign cost less than one hundred and fifty thousand dollars and I raised about half the money through the 'Dollars for Decency,' with people giving me a dollar or two because of my talkathon pleas. If I had had about ten thousand dollars in the bank when I started, I could have won because I would not have started our radio program so early," Faulkner believes.

The candidate felt he made two other tactical mistakes that also hurt his chances of winning.

"Jim Allen declared publicly that if he were not in the runoff, he would support me over Big Jim. The press and the Folsom people began demanding who I would support in the runoff. Naturally, I would state it over and over again, that was not a problem because if there were a runoff, I would be in it. Finally, Fred Taylor of the *Birmingham News,* who supposedly supported me, persuaded me to say that if I was not in the runoff, I would support Jim Allen. I should not have said this even though it was the way I felt. I admired Allen very much.

"The other tactical mistake I made was not having poll watchers. It may sound like sour grapes, but I found many incidents where votes were stolen from me or Jim Allen or others. Some of my friends even hired a detective who came up with proof of fraud, but I was not interested in contesting the election as I planned to run again in 1958. In fact, one of Folsom's big supporters later explained to me how this was done and admitted they had stolen enough votes to keep me from winning. Traditionally, in Alabama, a person had to run once 'to get ready to run' so he could be elected the second time. I also knew that people did not like, and I did not like, those who contested the results of an election. To me it was in poor taste and I did not contest it, thinking it would be my time in 1958. As a friend of mine said, 'I'll be late, but I'll be there in '58.'"

Governor's Race — 1958

Fueled by resistance to the federal government's school integration drive and probe of voter registration practices in the South, the race issue was thrust to the forefront in the 1958 governor's race, and it would remain there in subsequent campaigns into the 1970s. But a gangster shooting in Phenix City, Alabama, on June 18, 1954, wiping out the life of Albert Patterson, who had won the Democratic nomination for attorney general, would prove to be a deciding factor in this campaign.

Fourteen candidates lined up to vie for the state's top job in 1958, including several well-known former office holders. From the beginning, the favorites in the race seemed to narrow down to Jimmy Faulkner, runner-up in the previous race, John Patterson, who had been named by the Democratic Party to succeed his slain father as the state's attorney general in 1954, and George Wallace, a feisty circuit court judge from rural Barbour County.

"I knew that I was going to run in 1958, regardless of how I felt, because my friends would have convinced me that I had it in the bag," Faulkner remembers.

Under then-Alabama law, Jim Folsom could not succeed himself as governor, causing many to see Faulkner as the early favorite. After the 1954 election, however, Faulkner had put his political plans on hold in order to return to support his family and protect his business.

"Although I personally was willing to accept campaign funds, I refused to accept money to feed my family and run my daily operations so I went back to work. In the interim, I founded Loyal American Life Insurance Company, opening it July 4, 1955. I was able to raise 1.5 million dollars of investments for the company with ease. In fact, I sent back over a million dollars. This was a mistake because it made friends who got money back mad and later the company needed the money.

"Trying to make a living, I failed to keep up my contacts over the state because I did not have the time nor money to do so. This was a bad political error because by the time the next four years rolled around, many of my friends had committed to other candidates.

"George C. Wallace, for example, knew he was going to run and he worked almost day and night the entire three or four years before the '58 election.

"But the worse thing that happened to me, and actually the cause of my finally losing the election, was the slaying of Attorney General Elect-Albert Patterson."

John Patterson, who had been a partner in his father's law practice in Phenix City, was appointed to follow in his dad's steps as attorney general in the widely publicized clean-up of Phenix City. In 1956, he also had been successful in getting a state judge to issue an injunction against the NAACP to keep it from doing business in Alabama. In the governor's race, Patterson was quick to seize crime and race as issues, claiming the NAACP and organized crime were sending money to Alabama to defeat him. He also said he would get the legislature to pass a law that would force the closing of any Alabama schools integrated by the federal government.

Faulkner had a greater acceptance of integration than most Southerners, a trait that would work against him in a statewide election in the fifties.

"Race was very much an issue in this campaign. The Ku Klux Klan worked for John Patterson," Faulkner noted.

"As I have often stated, in the 1958 race if I had had another million dollars it would not have mattered, as I had plenty of money to run a decent campaign. I had a fine organization, the only mistake I made was running. I was the wrong candidate at the wrong time. The race issue took over, and I was not going to change. I think I was right, and time and circumstances have so proven. I was not going to pay that price.

"I have often thought that George Wallace was (later) willing to pay the price, and he's still paying it. I doubt that he would make the same decision if he had it to do over again. I guess he was a little hypocritical about it because he really did not hate blacks. The fact is, George was a very sympathetic person, and he had a kindly feeling for the downtrodden. He certainly was not the bombastic type fellow the public thought him to be."

Another factor that contributed to Faulkner's defeat was the entrance into the race of George Hawkins, Alabama Speaker of the House. He was an attorney for the labor unions and was well known in labor circles.

"I had the agreement with most organizations that I would be the only candidate endorsed by them. However, the Folsom people gave Hawkins forty thousand dollars to get him into the race. The unions could not pass him by, and they endorsed everybody except John Patterson. This gave John the best position, since labor was all divided and those opponents of labor were mostly united behind Patterson. He was in the best position by far."

When the votes were counted, Faulkner came in third behind Patterson and Wallace. In the runoff election, Patterson won convincingly over Wallace, who would never again be defeated in a governor's race in Alabama.

For Faulkner, the defeat was a blessing in disguise.

"Although I regretted losing these races for governor, it was an unusual experience. Fortunately, in both cases, I was one of the leading candidates and as a result, made many friends throughout Alabama, and many of those who are still living are still my friends, even though I am getting less and less known among the populace. As late as 1968 in a state-wide poll, my name was as well known in the state as George C. Wallace, and better than any single congressman in the state. That is no longer nearly true. In fact, now I can go places and not be recognized by most.

"As I have often said, before I was forty-two years old I had run for public office nine times, having won seven and lost two. And actually, the only two I won were the two I lost. I was fortunate not to have won the '58 election because from then on, for another twelve or fifteen years, race was the prominent issue and I did not fit into the issues of that period.

"Following the '58 race, financially, businesswise and otherwise, I had to make a new beginning. Although I had to struggle for a few years, I finally got over the hump with the help of a lot of friends and acquaintances."

The United States Senate — 1968

In 1968, many of Faulkner's friends tried to persuade him to run for the U.S. Senate. They even raised enough money to have a national firm conduct a poll to assess Faulkner's chances of winning.

"The poll indicated that I would have a hard time of it, but possibly could win. Amazingly, it showed that James B. Allen would lead the ticket against Armistead Selden. At that time, everybody thought Selden had the race in the bag.

"Allen had been calling me continuously, asking me for my

support. Finally, I told him that I would vote for him, but if he would follow my advice, I would work for him. He readily agreed and told me that I would make the difference in the campaign."

Faulkner gleaned the information received from pollster Oliver Quayle and came up with the formula for Allen's election: Allen would run against "that Washington Crowd."

"That slogan carried him through a hard-fought election and Allen won with less than a 5,000-vote majority. He gave me full credit for his election and he became the most popular political figure in Alabama for the last half of the twentieth century," Faulkner maintains.

In 1978, Jim Allen died suddenly while vacationing at his condominium in Gulf Shores. Faulkner and his wife, Evelyn, happened to be nearby and rushed to the vacation retreat.

"On Wednesday night before Jim Allen was buried, George Wallace called me and said, 'Jimmy, if you ask me, I'll appoint you United States Senator.' I thanked him but didn't accept it because I sincerely felt that Jim Allen wanted his wife to have it because his aide, Tom Coker, had told me that. Many years later I asked Coker who told him that Jim wanted his wife to succeed him? He replied, 'She did.'"

Some years before Allen's death, in 1972, Faulkner had considered running for Alabama's other U.S. Senate seat.

"I honestly believe that if I had done so, I would have been elected. Senator Allen, who was very popular, told me that if I would run he would be honored to have me as a fellow senator and that he would get out and publicly work for me. He said there was no other person in Alabama for which he would do that.

"In the meantime, George Wallace was shot, and he would have supported me, too. Even though I couldn't have won by myself, with these two I would have made it."

The question of whether Faulkner would run for the senate finally came down to a family issue. At the time, Faulkner's younger son, Wade, was a U.S. Navy ophthalmologist stationed in Phoenix, Arizona.

"Wade could not come home so Evelyn, Jimmy, Jr., and I got on a borrowed airplane and I flew the whole family out to see him. We had a family conference. Wade wanted me to run, Jimmy did not.

"Finally, Wade said, 'Well Jimmy, if Daddy runs, you will support him won't you?' to which Jimmy replied, 'Yes, I'll support him, and if my children get sick, I'll take them to the doctor, but I don't want them to get sick!'

"Jimmy won the argument, and I to this day have no regrets," Faulkner smiles.

When asked if he would have preferred to be governor or United States Senator, Faulkner quickly replies, "Senator."

"If I had been elected governor, I would only have been in office four years, with no continuity because of the race issue and the time in history. Serving as United States Senator has a possibility of continued service, and to me, offers many more interesting opportunities.

"I have been told many times by people from all areas of the state that if I had been elected governor in 1958, we would not have had the church bombing in Birmingham nor the Selma march. I admit that might be true, but I also admit that if that had been the case, I could not have been re-elected."

The George Wallace Connection

From the time of their trip together to the 1948 Democratic convention in Philadelphia, the political ride of Faulkner and George C. Wallace would sometimes be a bumpy one. In the fifties, they found themselves on different sides of the political fence. In the 1954 race for governor, Faulkner asked for Wallace's support.

"I went to see him in Clio. I was embarrassed because my pilot got lost, and Wallace waited out there on that little airfield an hour. But we went into town and I had lunch with him, Lurleen, and their oldest daughter, Bobbi. I asked him for his help and he said, 'Well, I've got to vote for Folsom because he gave me my technical schools, but I'm not going to do anything. That's all I'm going to do. I like you, and it would suit me to see you governor.'

"Well, the next week it came out that Wallace was Folsom's south Alabama campaign manager. I was pretty well teed off with him. But anyway, I paid him back in the 1958 runoff with Patterson. Patterson didn't have any campaign staff and nobody to raise his money, and I had a good organization; they just had the wrong candidate. My organization went in and raised the money for him in the runoff.

"Then in 1962, when George ran again, he told me, 'Jimmy, you claim that I cost you an election one time and I know that you cost me an election one time, can't we start all over again?'

"I said, 'Yeah.' So from then on we were friends. I don't think he really trusted me, though, until he ran the next time," Faulkner recalls.

Faulkner became a close friend, confidant and strong supporter of Wallace over the years. Wallace wanted to appoint Faulkner to his cabinet as director of the Alabama Development Office, the industry-hunting arm of state government.

"I appreciated the offer but had to turn it down. He asked me who I would recommend for the position and I told him, R. C. (Red) Bamberg. He and his staff laughed, but I told them he would make a good one. Red had wanted to be commissioner of prisons, and I told the governor, 'he's not mean enough for that.'

"Two or three years later I told Red what I had said and it made him mad. He said, 'I'm mean as hell!' And he would have been mean enough, but he did a great job at ADO," Faulkner laughs.

PRIOR TO THE 1966 governor's race, George Wallace had been unsuccessful in getting the legislature to pass a constitutional amendment that would have allowed a governor to succeed himself. The defeat upset Wallace, and Wallace's wife, Lurleen, ran for governor instead. She defeated nine other contenders, including two former governors and a former congressman, without a run-off. All during the campaign George Wallace made it clear that Lurleen's election would enable him to continue his national campaign activities in 1968. He had previously made creditable showings in Wisconsin, Indiana, and Maryland in the 1964 Democratic primaries.

In 1968, Wallace called on Faulkner to assist him in what columnist George Will described decades later as, "The most impressive eruption of popular participation in presidential politics since the Second World War . . . the most remarkably broad-based involvement that placed Wallace on all fifty state ballots, when impediments to ballot access for third parties were much more onerous than they are today."

To get on California's ballot, Wallace supporters had to gather 66,000 signatures, and each voter had to fill out a two-page, legal-size document of registration. "I went to California and was head of his campaign in Washington, Oregon, and California. Los Angeles was our headquarters, and I appeared on television against representatives for Nixon and Humphrey. I also appeared on television and put on a talkathon for him in Portland, Oregon, for twelve hours. In Oregon, he got a higher percentage of votes there than he got anywhere else in those three states," Faulkner boasts.

When the effort was ended, more than one hundred thousand had registered in the California campaign and ballot positions were secured. The Alabamian came in second in California. Wallace became the first third party candidate to gain ballot position in all fifty states. Although he did not gain the presidency, Wallace considered it a political victory that set the tone of presidential campaigns for years to come.

FAULKNER ALSO WAS CALLED upon to help Wallace regain the governor's office in 1970 from Albert Brewer. Wallace knew that his presidential hopes hinged on the governorship to provide a political platform for the future. Brewer, as Lieutenant Governor, had become governor upon the death of Lurleen Wallace, who was elected in 1966 when state law prohibited Wallace from seeking another term. As always, one of the most difficult tasks of any campaign is fund raising, and Wallace asked Faulkner to be his finance chairman, in addition to serving in his traditional role of political advisor.

The 1970 campaign set a benchmark for hard-fought, trench warfare in Alabama politics. Brewer and Wallace were the standouts in the seven-man primary. When the votes were counted, Brewer led Wallace 428,146 to 416,443. This set the stage for a hotly contested run-off. Charges and counter-charges were constant, race became a major issue, and Klan literature began to surface in highly populated areas of the state. It was, at times, an uncomfortable position for Faulkner, a racial moderate.

Brewer flooded the state with television commercials and print literature and it became obvious his campaign was well funded. Years later, Watergate testimony would reveal that four hundred thousand dollars was sent into the state from the Nixon forces seeking to defeat Wallace and keep him out of national politics.

However, raising money for Wallace was a tough task, and Faulkner had to co-sign a note for one hundred thousand dollars to keep the campaign alive.

Of even greater concern was the fact that polls showed Wallace trailing Brewer by 28 percent. Faulkner learned from contacts with pollsters that Brewer was capitalizing on Wallace's presidential ambitions with Brewer telling audiences that "I'll be a full-time governor." Wallace, meanwhile, was boasting of his 1968 turn-away crowds in Madison Square Garden and Detroit's Cobo Hall.

"I arranged a meeting with Wallace and talked to him as strongly as I have ever talked to anyone. I told him we were losing and that he had not convinced the people of Alabama that he wanted to be governor more than he wanted to be president. I told him to stop talking about national politics and pointed out that he had not mentioned God in any of his speeches. I told him to tell the people, 'With God's help, I'll make you a good governor,'" Faulkner admonished.

Wallace agreed, but told Faulkner, "Every time I try to mention God, I catch myself saying 'that G— D— *Birmingham News.*'"

The state's largest newspaper vehemently opposed Wallace in the campaign.

After Faulkner's meeting, Wallace changed his campaign speech. When the dust had settled in the run-off, he had out-distanced a bitter Brewer 559,832 to 525,951.

WITH THE STATE ELECTION out of the way, Wallace turned his attention again to presidential politics. This time, he would be involved in the Democratic primary.

Wallace's 1972 campaign was off to a roaring start. In the Florida primary, he carried every county in the state and forced rival candidate Hubert Humphrey to change his position on forced busing of school children. As expected, Wallace won big in states like North Carolina and Tennessee and won a plurality of Texas delegates. However, he surprised, or even shocked, political pundits with his second-place finish in Pennsylvania. He was on his way to victory in Michigan and Maryland when he was shot down by a would-be assassin on May 15 in Laurel, Maryland, one day before winning both states.

Shortly before the shooting, Humphrey had dispatched an emissary to probe Wallace's support. Insurance company mogul John Amos of Columbus, Georgia, contacted Faulkner on behalf of Humphrey to open a line of communication.

Was Humphrey willing to accept Wallace as a running mate should Humphrey receive the nomination?

Faulkner agreed to contact Wallace on May 19, but of course the plans were put on hold when the shooting occurred. On Wallace's third day in the hospital, Amos contacted Faulkner again saying Humphrey was ready to take Wallace on the ticket, "on crutches, in a wheelchair, or any way he could get him."

Faulkner passed the message on to Wallace on May 25 during a visit to Holy Cross Hospital in Silver Spring, Maryland. Wallace, whose body was riddled by five bullets, was still fighting for his life and would remain hospitalized until early July. Upon release, he flew in a government hospital plane for a brief stop in Montgomery before going on to the Democratic National Convention in Miami, where he would address the delegates on July 11.

"I went to the convention with the sole purpose of connecting Wallace with Humphrey," Faulkner said.

The Wallace campaign staff worked feverishly with candidate Henry Jackson's staff to try to block George McGovern's nomination. The question centered on the credentials committee's report regarding the seating of California's delegation. If the convention agreed to accept the committee's decision to divide California's delegates by popular vote, Humphrey could possibly win the nomination. However, Chairman Lawrence O'Brien, an open opponent of Wallace, ruled that the disputed delegates who favored Wallace and Humphrey would not be allowed to vote on the committee matter.

Meanwhile, Faulkner was meeting with Humphrey and his operatives to seal the alliance. Humphrey told Faulkner he wanted to contact three people before making the final arrangements, but noted that if the vote favored giving McGovern all of California's delegates, the battle would be lost.

O'Brien and his staff were working behind the scenes to convince delegates to vote to reject the committee's proposal. When the final votes were counted, McGovern won. But if O'Brien had not overlooked the rules and manipulated the delegates, McGovern would have been eleven votes short of an absolute majority and would have lost the California vote, allowing Humphrey to be the nominee.

"Frankly, if California could have been curtailed, Humphrey eventually would have been president because a Humphrey-Wallace ticket would have defeated Nixon. And Humphrey would not have lived to serve out a second term, so Wallace would have become President. But, of course, it was all over when they nominated McGovern," Faulkner opines.

McGovern suffered one of the worst defeats in U.S. political history.

Humphrey died of cancer in 1978.

AFTER AGONIZING IN PAIN for more than twenty-six years from the effects of five bullet wounds in Maryland, Wallace died in a Montgomery hospital September 13, 1998.

Thousands lined Dexter Avenue, leading to the State Capitol, for a last visit to the man nearly everyone in the state referred to as, "The Governor."

Faulkner received a special invitation to the funeral and sat in the historic Alabama House of Representatives Chamber in the Capitol for a service reserved for high state officials and special dignitaries. At this ceremony, the eulogy was delivered by former governor John Patterson. During the somber remarks, Patterson injected a note of bright reminiscence as he recounted the days that Wallace, Patterson, and Faulkner battled against each other in governor's races of the past. Patterson asked Faulkner to stand and be recognized, not just as a contender of Wallace, but as a special friend, as the three had become close in the years that had followed.

"Of course, I appreciated very much Patterson's kind words about me. It was pretty important to me because it identified me, first of all with Wallace and his family members who were there, and it also recognized that the three of us who led campaigns in '58 were still friends. I was full of appreciation.

"John Patterson and I became friends, as did John and George.

"I remember one time the three of us were out at the Patterson State Technical College in Montgomery to dedicate a building for my brother, Thurston. John, George and I were talking, and one of them said, 'Two of us were elected governor, and Jimmy beat us all because he's doing better than either of us.'"

AFTER ALL THESE YEARS, why does Jimmy Faulkner continue to be involved in politics? Is it for personal or business reasons?

"Well, there is no money in politics, really. But I must say that in the business I am in, the knowledge and personal acquaintance of people is helpful, and that's one reason to stay involved. People who are running for office come to see me, and personal contact is important to me, my engineering business, and it helps me get things for Baldwin County.

"I imagine over the years I have gotten ninety to a hundred million dollars of extra money for Baldwin County, and in our neighborhood re-development project, including housing and everything, over twelve million dollars. You've got to have contacts to do those things.

"For example, Governor George Wallace gave us money for land for a new school building out here, gave Perdido money, gave Elsanor money, drained highway 31, and gave a hundred and fifty thousand dollars to widen the Crossroads highway to four lanes. Actually, if we had not had the acquaintances, we wouldn't have the community college here," Faulkner asserts.

Is there a negative side to political involvement?

"Yes, on the negative side people think I can get jobs for them. A lot of times I can, but people have to realize that I am not an employment agency, and I ask my friends not to recommend me.

"Also, it's expensive. I guess I pay in contributions, travel and visitations fifteen thousand to twenty thousand dollars a year to keep up contacts. Much of it is now paid by the engineering company, but a lot is not. Like a few weeks ago, I was called to be a host at an event in north Alabama for a former senator who had been very good to me. I paid three thousand dollars and also hired an airplane for the trip just to do it.

"I don't know how many thousands of dollars I have given. I always get requests for contributions, and usually I try to do something, but I don't support more than one candidate in a race, with one exception. I did give money in the last governor's race to Don, because I felt close to him, while voting for Fob. I don't like to do this, but in this business, the governor is a powerful position, and in a business like mine, they can just ruin you in the last year of

office if they want to. Of course, Don is smart enough to realize
that, so I guess he doesn't hold it against me. You just get caught
from a lot of different angles."

Has he ever been tempted to say, "It's not worth it?"

"Well, I've said this. If I ever get to the point I can't help my
fellow man and do a service, I'm not worthy to be around. So, no,
I've never said it's not worth it.

"My greatest pleasure is not what I do for myself, it's what I do
for other people, and the Lord."

Making a living is important, but what is
far more important is learning how to live.

Jimmy Faulkner

12

Making a Living

R unning for office and losing is not a profitable enterprise. Following his race for governor in 1954, Jimmy Faulkner knew he had to come up with some way to make a living for his family. Two of his friends, Jimmy Folmar and Henry Flinn, suggested he start an insurance business.

"I took their advice and began making a study of it and decided to start a company in Mobile. I decided on the name Loyal American Life Insurance Company, as I liked the words 'loyal' and 'American,' thus combining them into what was an ideal name.

"We decided to capitalize the company with a sale of $1.5 million in stock. Amazingly, I was able to sell about $2.5 million without commissions or anything. Unwisely, we decided to give $1 million back as we thought we would only need $1.5 million as we originally planned. That turned out to be a mistake because with expanding business we needed the extra money and we also made a lot of friends mad by returning their money. The stock went up rather rapidly for a spell and they felt deprived of the profit," Faulkner remembers.

But Faulkner was not experienced in the insurance business

and relied heavily on people who were not much better. The company began to decline but Faulkner, who had been runner-up for governor, felt it would be better businesswise, and otherwise, if he continued to run the company of which he was chairman of the board and CEO. He also was receiving a good salary, for that time, of twenty-five thousand dollars a year, plus stock options.

When it came decision time for the 1958 governor's race, Faulkner was tempted to remain with the insurance company.

"However, friends of mine had put in a lot of time, energy and money in my gubernatorial campaign and it would have been a catastrophe so far as friendships were concerned, had I not run in 1958. I felt that running for governor and continuing to operate the insurance company would be unwise, so I sold my interest in the insurance business."

Before leaving, Faulkner had employed Matthew S. Metcalfe, a young man who at the time was working for the Alabama State Docks, who proved to be a brilliant learner and rapidly became knowledgeable of the insurance business. He eventually became president and CEO, building the company to more than two hundred million dollars in assets.

Metcalfe eventually sold the company and, during the past several years, the headquarters was moved from Mobile, a sad day for Faulkner and others associated with the company's beginning.

"Naturally, I think sometimes if I had stuck to the insurance business and made a go of it, I would be much better off financially now. However, I have no regrets because I was able to get into other enterprises and at the same time ran for governor. Even though I did lose that race, I did make many lasting friends, and that has been worth more than anything else," Faulkner concludes.

Newspapers

During the period of 1936 through 1974, Faulkner had been owner or part owner of six newspapers, all located in south Alabama. These included his home newspaper, the *Baldwin Times*, along with the *Atmore Advance*, the *Monroe Journal* in Monroeville, the *South Alabamian* in Jackson, the *Onlooker* in Foley and the *Fairhope Courier*. In 1941 Faulkner was elected president of the Alabama Press Association at the age of twenty-six, the youngest in the nation.

Faulkner at first turned down the offer from the E. B. Gaston family to buy the Fairhope newspaper, explaining that he did not feel one person should own all the newspapers in one county. Later, however, he decided to purchase the paper from Berkley Thompson of Mobile, who had bought it from the Gastons. Eventually, he sold his interest in the *Advance, Monroe Journal* and *South Alabamian*.

While Faulkner owned the Baldwin County newspapers and while Jack House and Steve Mitchell were editors of the *Times*, John Cameron was editor of the *Onlooker* and Mike and Linda Breedlove were in charge of the *Courier*.

"Every paper I had an interest in received numerous awards, and at one time or another each paper won 'Number One in Alabama' in its category and top in General Excellence. In 1967 the *Baldwin Times* was selected to receive the 'Lurleen B. Wallace' award which was engraved, 'Alabama Press Association — Governor Lurleen B. Wallace trophy 1967 presented to the *Baldwin Times.*' This was the only award ever given by Governor Lurleen B. Wallace as she died soon thereafter," Faulkner recalls.

Later, Faulkner's son, Jimmy, as part owner, handled the day-to-day operations of the Baldwin County newspapers until the

Faulkners finally decided in the seventies to sell all three properties to newspapermen Frank Helderman, Sr., and Frank Helderman, Jr., of Gadsden, Alabama.

Faulkner had always written a weekly column and insisted to the new owners that he be retained as a paid columnist. This allowed him to continue to have a voice in the happenings of his community and the county while earning an extra hundred dollars per month.

"I just enjoy writing. I always have since I was about twenty years old. I used to write a column called 'Byways of Baldwin,' a personal column, then I went off into the war. When I came back, I started a column called 'Mumblings,' with the idea that I would talk about several subjects in each column.

"Now, mostly I write about traveling. I found that I could write about politics or government and I would hardly hear from anyone. But when I would write about the Amazon, Alaska or some place like that, I would get responses from a lot of people, especially elderly people. They would say, 'I read your column. Where are you going next?'" Faulkner smiles.

Does the constant exposure and being in the public spotlight cause any problems for Faulkner?

"Well, I will never forget when I bought the *Baldwin Times* from Mr. Vail, he said, 'Jimmy, remember that the higher you get up the pole, the more people will throw rocks at you. They don't throw rocks down, they throw them up.' And I guess that may be somewhat true."

"Turn Your Radio On"

In the mid-1950s, television was new to most rural areas with families staring at snowy screens, often straining to detect fading images of their favorite shows. But radio was more popular than ever. It was the era that saw the debut of hip-twisting Elvis Presley while other popular artists like Frank Sinatra, Dean Martin, Eddie Fisher, Patti Page, and Jo Stafford filled the airwaves with their recordings.

When Herbert Hoover was Secretary of Commerce, the rules for owning a radio station were outlined in the 1927 Radio Act. In exchange for a license to operate a radio station, operators would pledge to devote a designated amount of the airtime to local news, public service programs, and community affairs. Owners were limited to the number of stations they could operate, and no two AM stations of one owner could be so close as to overlap their signals.

During the deregulation era of the Reagan Administration, things were changed. And the rules have changed even more recently so that a license to operate a station may now go to the highest bidder, with the money going into the nation's treasury. Now, one media company may own hundreds of stations, even several within a single metropolitan area, with almost any type of programming format.

But that was not the case in the 1950s when stations were required to operate "in the public interest, convenience, and necessity." Baldwin County had only one radio station, WHEP in Foley, in the south end of the county. The call letters represented the initials of the majority owner, Howard E. Pill, although at the time station personnel joked privately that they stood for "We Hate Elvis Presley." The station was first managed by Pill's son-in-law, Ralph Howard, and the program manager was a young graduate of the University of Alabama, Jim Stewart.

In 1957, Jimmy Faulkner felt that Bay Minette also should have a radio station. Faulkner, Pill, and Stewart applied with the Federal Communications Commission (FCC) for a license for a one thousand-watt AM station and they called it WBCA, which stood for "Wonderful Baldwin County Alabama."

Pill also owned a station in Georgia and decided to sell his interest in the two Baldwin County stations to Faulkner and Stewart so that he could spend more time with the Georgia station. Faulkner owned 75 percent of the stations and Stewart held 25 percent.

Soon, Faulkner wanted to branch out and the group purchased a station in Bremen, Georgia. When further stations were considered, Stewart decided he wanted to stay with the local station in Foley.

"Jim is one of the best small market radio station operators in Alabama," Faulkner said, "but he was more interested in immediate profits than delayed capital expansions."

Given the choice of Bremen or Foley, Stewart bought total interest in the south Baldwin station in Foley, which he has called home ever since. The thousand-watt AM station has proved quite successful for Stewart and his family over the years.

Later, Faulkner added an FM station in Bay Minette.

Meanwhile, Faulkner and newspaper publisher Bill Stewart in Monroeville decided to build a radio station in that town. Faulkner had once hired Stewart at the *Baldwin Times* in Bay Minette and later the two had purchased the *Monroe Journal*, which Stewart operated.

"That radio venture proved very profitable. The Monroeville station cost about twenty-one thousand dollars for building, land, equipment, and license and it paid for itself in about twenty months," Faulkner remembers.

Meanwhile, the operator of Faulkner's Bremen, Georgia, station, Bob Thorburn, was given and sold a fifteen percent interest in Faulkner Radio, Inc., and the corporation purchased the FM and AM stations in Carrollton, Georgia. It was one of the finest operations in northwest Georgia. The corporation had to sell Bremen before purchasing Carrollton because of the proximity, as the FCC at that time would not permit ownership of both.

"Bob was a good operator and made progress, so we then built new stations, FM and AM, in the Auburn/Opelika area," Faulkner said.

This gave the corporation a total of seven stations. At this time, Faulkner owned 75 percent of the stations, Thorburn 15 percent, and the remainder was held by Faulkner's two sons and his executive assistant, Dorothy Martin, and her husband, Albert.

In 1970, two lawyers decided to build a station in Carrollton to compete with Faulkner and Thorburn. Thorburn contested their plans.

"Bob was the general manager of all the stations. He got into some trouble with the FCC over the Carrollton issue that resulted in complicated litigation that lasted twelve years and cost more than two hundred thousand dollars in legal fees. Finally, he was forced to sell his interest, which I bought," Faulkner added.

Faulkner's radio involvement spanned nearly half a century.

"Even though radio stations are relatively simple to operate, compared to newspapers, I was not a radio man and did not figure my qualifications adequate to continue operating them, even though I was able to get managers," Faulkner observes.

"The Auburn/Opelika stations were profitable and later the corporation purchased Cedartown, Georgia, which was always a profitable station. We paid two hundred thousand dollars for it and it paid for itself right away," Faulkner added.

Faulkner said he decided to gradually dispose of his interest in radio stations because of his advancing age, and he felt it was time for him to begin getting his business affairs in more liquid shape. However, he asserts that selling radio and TV properties are more

complicated than most businesses because the transactions must
be approved by the FCC.

"I gave the Carrollton FM station and the Cedartown stations
to Faulkner University and then sold the Auburn/Opelika stations
to Gary Fuller, who is also a great radio operator.

"Fuller purchased the stations at $950,000 and never missed a
payment. He later sold them for about $3 million. They were very
successful," Faulkner stated.

Faulkner later sold his Bay Minette AM station, WBCA, to local
businessman Gordon Earls, and he in turn sold it again.

"That left me only the FM station in Bay Minette, which we
were able to get the power increased to six thousand watts and we
moved the operation to Mobile. Finally, after experimenting with
different formats and getting a new manager, it was doing well.
Then, Tim Camp and Ken Johnson wanted to buy it so, in 1998, I
sold it and that ended my radio business," Faulkner said.

"Actually, I have invested comparatively little cash money in
purchasing the various stations, having an interest in nine all
together, off and on, but finally sold them or gave them away at a
nice profit," Faulkner recalls.

The Bay Minette/Mobile FM station which now has a sports
format is doing well and proving very successful for new owners.
WNSP is worth much more than when he sold it.

"Being a trained newspaper man, I never really liked the radio
business as well as I did newspapers . . . I enjoyed the radio business,
but frankly, made the most money by selling them. Radio properties sell for amazing prices, as it seems some people want to own
them for the prestige while others are able to make them into very
profitable businesses.

"Having the only station in a town of from ten thousand to
twenty thousand population is a good property and, properly run,

can make a good profit, while at the same time, serve the local community well," Faulkner concluded.

Other Business

Over the years Faulkner has entered into various other business endeavors, including timberlands and other property. In 1975, he became partner in a chemical plant.

"Jack Boykin came to see me about putting a chemical plant in Bay Minette. It was obvious he was well versed in the chemical business. About all he had was a good idea and I eventually agreed to finance the proposal by borrowing money at the First National Bank in Mobile. We erected the plant on Highway 225 and CSX Railroad at Carpenter Station six miles west of Bay Minette.

"The operation was never very big, but had its ups and downs. We eventually borrowed two million dollars from the Farmers Home Administration to expand and continue operations.

"In the meantime, Jack and I decided if someone wanted to pay our price, we would sell it. Uniroyal expressed an interest through a mutual friend. Jack and I went to New York and made them a proposal, which they accepted," Faulkner said.

The venture turned out profitably. Boykin and Faulkner owed about three million dollars on the plant. They asked for seven million and, to their surprise, Uniroyal accepted.

"Here again, I knew practically nothing about the chemical business," Faulkner declares.

I never spend any time getting even . . . I know that in most cases, what goes around comes around. I leave getting even up to the Good Lord.

Jimmy Faulkner

13

Volkert & Associates

The unsuccessful 1958 governor's race convinced Jimmy Faulkner that he needed to change directions in his life. He wanted to be governor all right, but he did not have that burning, churning obsession in the pit of his stomach that some other political candidates suffered, day and night. It's an affliction that knows no cure other than total commitment and dedication of mind, body and resources toward political success.

Faulkner had dedicated his financial savings to the campaign and was "pretty broke."

"I needed to get into something to help earn a living. Jimmy Jr., was back from college, ready to operate the *Baldwin Times* and the newspaper was hardly large enough to provide a comfortable living for two families.

"E. E. (Bill) Delaney of Mobile, who had been one of the directors of Loyal American Life Insurance Company, suggested I contact David Volkert of Ewin Engineering Company as he could probably use someone like me to help build his company," Faulkner remembered.

Volkert had purchased Ewin Engineering in 1954 from Captain Ed Roberts of Waterman Steamship Company and was operating it from offices in Mobile and newly opened offices in Miami. In its earlier days in New Orleans the firm had specialized in waterfront engineering. During World War II, emphasis shifted entirely to military projects. Over the years, the firm has established an outstanding record in designing bridges, highways, airports, stadiums, and other engineering projects. In 1963 the name was changed to David Volkert & Associates. In 2000, Volkert was listed as one of the top two hundred design firms in the United States.

When Faulkner decided to place his phone call to Volkert in 1958, little did he realize that his action would lead to both the highest peak of his financial success as well as the lowest valley of professional crisis he would face in his life.

"David had been one of my loyal supporters in politics. I learned that he was in Miami and I called him and told him that he might need somebody like me in his engineering company. He invited Evelyn and me to fly down at his expense to discuss the matter.

"He met us at the airport and we discussed business about ten minutes. He offered me a proposal on a commission basis with a $1,400 a month retainer. That just happened to be, at the time, the minimum I needed," Faulkner recalled.

The new employee worked for a year and a half before he was finally earning enough to warrant the retainer. But then, good things began to happen.

"David told me that over the past five years the company had averaged $250,000 a year in fees. He said that as long as I could keep it up to that point, I did not need to worry about a job. Before long, I had the income up to one million dollars, then up to two million, and then three million. At that point, he decided I was making more on my commissions than the company was earning and that

I should be put on a salary, which I agreed," Faulkner smiled.

"I was fairly successful in my promotion of the firm because of the many friends I had made over the state and I had a rather good reputation," Faulkner added.

Through his political involvement Faulkner had made many friends, not only in Alabama but also in Louisiana, where Volkert had its initial roots. The Louisiana contacts included his old friend, Governor Jimmie Davis, and governors succeeding him.

In 1983, David Volkert began to think about retiring and decided to sell the company to the employees under an ESOP, a method whereby employees could acquire a company over a period of years.

"He agreed to sell it to us for three million dollars and we had about ten years in which to pay for it. Business continued to improve and from 1958, beginning with eight or ten employees, the company kept growing under the able leadership of Keith King, who became President and CEO in 1983, with many other able engineers, such as Charles Munden, who with myself are the two senior employees," Faulkner said.

The company continued its steady growth with offices in Mobile and Birmingham; New Orleans; Tampa and Ft. Walton Beach; Chattanooga; and Alexandria, Virginia, and field offices in several other locations.

King has attributed much of the firm's rapid success to Faulkner.

"Jimmy is a great asset to our firm. I have known him for about forty years, so I believe I can speak from experience. He is distinguished by his hard work and tenacity, and his ability to follow through on a project to its completion. If he runs into a roadblock, he just backs up and comes from another direction until he can find a resolution.

"He is dedicated to his family and to his church, but he doesn't try to force his religion on others. He demonstrates his faith through his example and the way he lives," King said.

Faulkner, who has worked for years now with this engineering firm, is not an engineer. Has this been a drawback to Volkert?

"No. He never passes himself off as an engineer. He is quick to identify himself as who he is, and he tells a client that if they need to talk to an engineer, he will get one from the firm to talk to them.

"Jimmy is, I guess you would say, a salesman. And he's good at it! He's been very successful," King adds.

In the year 2000, the company celebrated its seventy-fifth anniversary with a goal of fifty million dollars in sales for the year. Faulkner is the senior employee of the company, both in age and in time of service.

"The connection with Volkert has been a good thing for me and I have enjoyed it. Although I am one of the largest stockholders of the company, my percentage of the firm is very small, as is the case with all other employees.

"As long as I feel I am maintaining good health and earn my keep, I have no plans to retire. Of course, at age eighty-five, I have no perception of how much longer my health will permit me to put forth the sometimes strenuous efforts it takes to obtain the business and be worth my salt," Faulkner concludes.

"Climbing Crisis Mountain"

Building the world's longest bridge turned out to be the hardest personal mountain Faulkner would climb in his professional life. It began in late 1964 when David Volkert discovered that a twenty-four-mile bridge would be built across Lake Pontchartrain outside New Orleans to connect the port city to St. Tammany Parish. Landing the engineering contract on such a monumental under-taking would not only be a feather in the cap of Volkert Engineering, but would vault the firm's reputation to a new national height.

Faulkner was assigned the task of making the initial contacts in hopes of obtaining the project. As usual, his "salesman" efforts were successful, but years later he would pay a terrific price.

In 1973, the New Orleans bureau of the Associated Press released a story that would draw banner headlines in Louisiana, as well as Alabama. The AP reported that Faulkner, identified as a close friend of Alabama Governor George Wallace, was one of five persons, including Volkert and Andrew Erwin, indicted on charges of bribery to influence public officials in the awarding of the multi-million dollar contract. The story claimed Faulkner received two hundred thousand dollars, which represented ten percent of the two million dollar engineering fees. The AP claimed that Faulkner was to give ten percent of the money to former St. Tammany Parish Sheriff Erwin, who in turn would give ten percent of what he received to a former member of the New Orleans Expressway Commission, Ira Champagne. Both Erwin and Champagne were named as co-conspirators.

The AP story said the indictment alleged other conspiracies involving Angelo Bosco, a member of the commission, and Bosco's brother, Samuel, both of Slidell, Louisiana. A former state representative, Jessie D. McClain, also was indicted for allegedly receiving payment from Erwin.

The U.S. Attorney, Gerald J. Gallinghouse, maintained that Faulkner actually received four hundred thousand dollars and paid two hundred and fifty thousand dollars to Erwin, who allegedly then paid twenty thousand to McClain, twenty thousand to the Boscos, and twenty thousand to Winnie Champagne, the widow of then deceased Champagne.

Faulkner was quick to admit that a payment of two hundred fifty thousand dollars was made to Erwin, but maintained that it was a legitimate fee, necessary to work through the web of obtaining special legislation, legal matters, disposition of bonds in a tight bond market, and other such barriers. He blamed the indictment on an ongoing effort by the Nixon administration to discredit George Wallace who was at the height of his political popularity, and a serious threat to Nixon's political career.

"Watergate testimony has since revealed that Nixon directed at least four hundred thousand to Wallace's opponent, Albert Brewer, in the 1970 governor's race to end Wallace's political career and to keep him from running for president in 1972. Further evidence also came out that Nixon sent dozens of FBI agents into Alabama to investigate Wallace, his campaign leaders, and major contributors. Nixon even ordered the Justice Department to investigate the tax returns of close Wallace associates," Faulkner said.

Faulkner further pointed out that he was the primary political target of the New Orleans investigation as Gallinghouse offered immunity to everybody else indicted in the case (and also offered immunity to Volkert) if they would testify against Faulkner.

"Gallinghouse even offered immunity to Erwin, the man who actually handled the payments. But I was never offered any kind of immunity," Faulkner affirms.

Faulkner said that everybody turned down the U.S. Attorney's offer of immunity except Erwin, whose testimony remained the same after the agreement was made to not prosecute him.

"Gallinghouse knew all along he did not have a case. There was simply no evidence to warrant prosecution. Erwin even testified that I knew nothing of what he had done," Faulkner said.

Faulkner later obtained a copy of a letter Gallinghouse had written March 29, 1974, to the Justice Department in Washington. The U.S. Attorney recommended that proceedings against all defendants in the case be dismissed, but Faulkner was not informed of this decision. The following year, a federal judge ordered the court to expunge Faulkner's name from all records. To this date there is no court record of the entire years-long proceedings that was a prolonged nightmare for Faulkner.

"It cost a lot of money to fight the indictment, and it caused a lot of heartache for me and embarrassment to my family, but there was some good to come out of it as well," Faulkner assures.

During the course of the event, Wallace spoke out for Faulkner in Alabama, confirming the case was part of a Nixon witch hunt. Faulkner's dear friend, U. S. Senator Jim Allen, offered to be a character witness. Former Louisiana Governor Jimmie Davis called to assure Faulkner that his friends would be even closer now than ever before. Alabama friends from Mobile to Florence called to express their friendship and support.

"It was a very uplifting experience to have so many people contact me to express their feelings. Such friendship will be remembered much longer than the harassment of political adversaries," Faulkner affirms.

After the case had been dismissed, Faulkner thought it was all over. That was not the case. The Internal Revenue Service got into the act and claimed Faulkner owed four hundred thousand dollars in taxes.

"I hired able accountants and attorneys, but they would not listen to reason. They released to the press that I had wrongly tried to avoid paying income taxes.

"This gave me a good lesson about the IRS and their devious ways of getting money. Every now and then they would release another story about my owing the money. I appealed the case to one of their judges, who was employed by the IRS. These judges are nothing but tax collectors themselves," Faulkner explains.

Finally the IRS reduced the charges to forty thousand dollars.

By then, the case had become a real nuisance and aggravation, not only to Faulkner but also to the firm.

"I wanted to continue fighting the case but David Volkert, president and owner of the engineering company, said he was tired of seeing it played up in newspapers. He said that he would pay the money they claimed I owed and just let it drop. Reluctantly, I did this. About all I got out of it was a good lesson on how crooked and unfair the IRS can be.

"Later, one of their agents apologized to me saying he did not realize certain facts in the case, even though those facts were in his hands all the time."

Faulkner said he also learned that one cannot appeal a case to the civil courts unless he paid the amount claimed, and then sue to get it back. In his case it would have taken four hundred thousand in cash and probably years to resolve the matter. He said that unlike other cases, the burden of proof is on the accused, not the accuser.

Did Faulkner take any action in trying to get even with Gallinghouse for the injustice?

"My philosophy on that is that I never spend any time getting even. I try to spend all my time trying to help somebody. I know that in most cases, what goes around comes around. I leave getting even up to the Good Lord," Faulkner replied.

Some time after the dust had settled in the New Orleans case, Gallinghouse was considered for appointment to one of two vacancies for federal judgeships. Faulkner later learned that the U.S. attorney failed to be appointed because of his mishandling of matters in the alleged bribery case.

Another Lawsuit

In October of 1980, Faulkner was again struck with unfavorable newspaper publicity as a result of a lawsuit. On the front page of the Sunday edition of the *Mobile Press Register* was the headline, "Bank, Faulkner Linked in Land Deal."

The story, written by Chip Drago, stated that "James H. Faulkner of Bay Minette is being sued for $8.6 million."

Being sued is not an every day occurrence for anyone, but a small amount may not have ensured such big headlines.

The article stated: "Mushrooming litigation linking a Mississippi executive, Mobile's largest bank, a political kingmaker in Baldwin County and a floundering contracting firm sprouted Friday in Vicksburg, Miss."

The article continued, "In Warren County Chancery Court, Bernie B. Bierman of Greenville, Miss., filed an $8.6 million suit against Bay Minette-based business tycoon James H. Faulkner for the role the Alabamian allegedly played in appropriating real estate valued 'in the neighborhood of $2 million.'"

Bierman accused Merchants National Bank of Mobile, Ball-Co Contractors, Inc., and Faulkner of "fraud, misrepresentation and deceit."

In a matter of days, the Mississippi courts threw out the case because it had no foundation.

What was Faulkner's reaction to the suit?

"Being a newspaper man myself, I have strong feelings about the press printing factual and fair stories. This was neither."

"Interestingly, neither Mr. Drago nor the *Press Register* ever reported the fact that the case was thrown out of court. Within several months, the person doing the suing was put in prison, accused of fraud.

"Some investigative reporters are on the lookout for a startling headline and news and don't care who is hurt. In journalism school, such people are referred to as journalism prostitutes."

A state does not spend money for education. It invests its money and that investment yields the highest income return of any investment a state can make. Sense in children's heads is worth more than dollars in safety vaults.

Governor Bibb Graves
1939 Address to Alabama Legislature

14

Education

When Jimmy Faulkner was a teenage boy, he helped his mother pack up their 1928 Chevrolet and they headed out to New Mexico. It proved more than just an adventure for the young man; it was a dose of reality. New Mexico had better schools and better pay for teachers. Jimmy, at fifteen, entered his senior year of high school while his mother worked to complete her college degree. Jimmy's older brother, Thurston, had finished two years of college in New Mexico and made more money as a beginning teacher in Silver City than their mother, with her years of teaching experience, had ever made in Alabama.

Even at that early age, Faulkner discovered that classes in New Mexico were more difficult than those in his home state and the schools were better. Entering high school there, all students were given an IQ test.

"The principal, 'Pop' Amy, called me to his office and said, 'James, did you know you made the highest score in school on your IQ test?' I replied, 'No, I didn't.' Naturally I felt proud. Then, he gave it to me . . . 'But your grades don't show it'."

Jimmy's father and mother both had insisted that the boys get the best education possible, including going to college.

"There was nothing except that we would be educated. So I think that it was my family's influence that sparked my interest in education, and I was also inspired by the fact that my mother, who taught school for thirty-nine years, never made as much as one thousand dollars a year teaching. It was through her meager salary that we were able to exist, and when she died she had absolutely no retirement," Faulkner remembers.

"Back then, when we lived on the farm, the school term was only three months long the first year she taught. That was a typical school year. Then, it gradually got up to five months, and some thought that was horrible. In 1926, Bibb Graves campaigned for governor on a pledge of providing a seven-month term his first year and an eight-month term the second year. When it increased to seven months, the farmers really objected because it deprived them from having good farm labor out of their children," Faulkner remembers.

In 1920, the average school term in Alabama was 123 days, compared to a national average of 162 days. The average teacher's salary that year was $484, compared to $871 nationally. Of course, the Great Depression hit in 1929 and many Alabama teachers were paid little or nothing. The average teacher pay in 1932 was actually less than it was in 1920. It was not until many years later that the school year increased to nine months.

"So I guess the plight of teachers and the fact that we in Alabama were getting an inferior education compared to New Mexico, for example, influenced my early interest in improving education, improving the retirement program, and giving Social Security to our teachers and our state employees," Faulkner adds.

For the Faulkner family, education was always a family matter, although his father did not receive much formal education.

"My dad probably did not go through the fourth or fifth grade, but he had a lot of common sense and was a successful farmer. My mother began teaching school out of high school and her first year she taught three months making twenty-five dollars per month and paying five dollars of that for room and board.

"She was determined to get a college education and took all kinds of correspondence courses, went to summer school when possible and struggled over thirty years to finally get her A.B. degree at the same time I graduated from high school in Silver City, New Mexico. We were on the graduation stage together since the high school and the college were on the same campus," Faulkner recalls.

After high school, Faulkner attended Freed-Hardeman College in Henderson, Tennessee. During his two years there, he earned one hundred dollars doing public relations work for the school and the remainder of the $250-per-year-cost came from his mother, a few dollars per month.

"My brother had gone to school for two years, both at the University of Alabama and Silver City State Teachers College in New Mexico. To help my mother and me, he quit school. But after I graduated from college, my brother and his wife, Odette, struggled and he got his bachelors degree in Agriculture at Mississippi State, later receiving his masters at Auburn University," Faulkner adds.

Thurston was principal of a rural Mississippi high school and later taught vocational agriculture at Fayette, Alabama. He was promoted by Auburn to be Future Farmers of America (FFA) director for the entire state. Later he became a district agent for vocational education and finally was promoted through the merit system to become State Director of Vocational and Higher Education. He was not only head of the vocational and technical schools in Alabama but also the two-year colleges.

After he retired from state service, he became Executive Vice

President of Alabama Christian College in Montgomery.

"Adding it all together, my family spent seventy-five years working for education, my mother and brother working professionally, with me as a worker on the sidelines," Faulkner concludes.

This does not include his support and work on behalf of the Christian university named in his honor, as outlined earlier.

AFTER FAULKNER'S successful campaign for state senate in 1950, Lieutenant Governor Jim Allen named him chairman of the Education Committee. Fifteen years earlier the legislature had enacted the Minimum Program Act, thought to be a model equity plan for the entire nation. Its purpose was to ensure that every child receive equal access to education, regardless of area of residency in the state. Because of flaws in the program, different property valuations and assessments in various counties, it had to be revised in 1939. Still, it was too complicated.

"One of the problems with the Minimum Program Act was that nobody could understand it. It had so many complexities that probably no more than two or three people in Alabama could understand it. I tried to simplify it," Faulkner said.

Faulkner worked with a financial representative of the governor's office, an expert on loan from the University of Alabama, and with J. H. Hadley of Tuscaloosa, president of the Alabama Education Association and brother of John Hadley of Bay Minette.

"We all studied it, made changes, and the minimum program became the basis for channeling millions of dollars to local school systems in the state.

"And something that evolved as an outcome of that study was a realistic teacher retirement program and the inclusion of Alabama teachers in the Social Security program," Faulkner recalled.

Although a law authorizing a retirement system for teachers was actually passed by the legislature in 1939, it lacked funding and could not grant benefits as no funds were available. Faulkner worked with Hadley and others to develop a comprehensive retirement program that was passed by the legislature, almost entirely as written, in the 1953 session.

At this time, teachers were not eligible for coverage under Social Security. Faulkner's committee pushed legislation in 1951 to allow coverage as soon as the federal law was amended. Then in 1953, the same law setting up the retirement system also provided the funding for teachers to receive Social Security once the federal legislation was in place. Finally, in 1954, President Dwight D. Eisenhower signed the law authorizing coverage for teachers on a state-by-state basis, and Alabama teachers were ready and eager to take advantage of this benefit.

"Because we had passed legislation, we were the first state in the nation to provide Social Security for our teachers and our state employees, and we did it by keeping retirement and Social Security separate so that retired teachers would receive two checks.

"Today, Alabama's state retirement system is recognized everywhere as the best in the nation," Faulkner declares.

Faulkner also worked with Hadley and his organization in defending Alabama's teacher tenure law that was in jeopardy. The law came under attack in the legislature in 1951, and again in a legislative interim committee hearing in 1952. School board members felt the law made it too difficult to fire incompetent teachers. Faulkner helped fashion a compromise on the matter in the 1953 session.

Faulkner's support for education was a major factor in his being named Outstanding Freshman Senator by the Capitol Press Corps.

The Community College System

Faulkner has become perhaps the strongest advocate of Alabama's community college system, taking on its most vocal critics at every opportunity. He has termed the establishment of the two-year colleges "the greatest advancement in education during the last half of the twentieth century." He has reason to be proud.

"I was the first one to ever mention such a system statewide, when I ran for governor in 1958. I was somewhat acquainted with the California system, which really just added two years to various high schools. That was frankly my kind of idea, which we could afford to do that without a lot of expense and a lot of buildings. Of course, I did not get elected, but I did get interested in it, I was advocating it and I saw a great need for it. Then in 1962, George Wallace took it up and brought it to fruition.

"There was a great hue and cry by the *Birmingham News*, the *Mobile Register*, and the *Montgomery Advertiser*. They talk about too many two-year colleges, they don't listen to any arguments or discussion but just make flat statements as if they know what they were talking about, which they don't," Faulkner assures.

One of the arguments advanced by the daily newspapers was that the institutions were placed politically.

"Well, George Wallace's idea was to put them within fifty miles of everybody in the state. To do that, you have to divide them geographically, whether it's political or whatever it is. But every institution in Alabama was put where it was politically, with the possible exceptions of the University of South Alabama in Mobile and UAB in Birmingham. They were something that just had to be, sooner or later.

"But the University of Alabama was established back in 1835, and Auburn somewhat later, then the so-called 'Normal' schools, the two-year schools in Florence, Livingston, Daphne, Troy, and Jacksonville, were put politically because of distribution in the various areas.

"Why did they put the University of Alabama in Tuscaloosa, and why did they put Auburn in Auburn? It was political, because the rural areas distrusted the cities. And the rural areas at that time dominated the legislature. So the legislature absolutely would not consider putting a university in Birmingham or Montgomery where the big mules were. So, it was political! And I don't know anything much that happens that is not political," Faulkner concludes.

About 1960, Governor John Patterson appointed a blue ribbon committee to select sites for six proposed junior colleges in Alabama. Dr. Howell Hadley, a native of Baldwin County and brother of the chairman of the county commission, was a member of this committee. Bay Minette was selected as one of these six sites but nothing was ever done to build the college.

In 1964, the state legislature passed a bill to build ten junior colleges in the state. This time, Bay Minette was determined to get one of these ten. Faulkner tells how this came about.

"There were nine members of the state board and each member got a college for his district. The member representing our district lived in Monroeville so that town got a college, and I didn't think that was right. So, I went around and got a meeting called and we met in the city hall courtroom. I told them we ought to go for it, and do everything we could.

"They said, 'Well, Monroeville already has it.' I said, 'Well, that's true, but maybe there will be another one.'

"So, we decided to raise five thousand dollars to make a promotional film and support the effort. They wanted me to be chairman and I agreed, providing they would make L. D. (Dick) Owen co-chairman. He was in the state senate at the time and was a very close friend of Governor Wallace.

"We made the film and businessman Albert Thompson and some others went to Montgomery to the board meeting. We really went all out to get a college here. Fairhope was trying to get it, and they were talking about what a beautiful place Fairhope would be for a college and that they ought to have it. But that's all they did, they just talked.

"The board had prepared cubby holes for each town to put its information and materials. Fairhope had one page and we had ours full of different information.

"When all was said and done, Governor George Wallace promised me that he would give us a junior college. In the meantime, Brewton had gotten one, so we were going to have to be the third one in this district.

"Eventually, Dick Owen and I went before the State Board of Education. Dr. Austin Meadows was State Superintendent of Education and he brought up the matter. Dr. Harold Martin of Birmingham, a Methodist Bishop, made the motion that Bay Minette be given a junior college, and George Wallace seconded the motion. It was carried unanimously.

"As an afterthought, Dr. Meadows said, 'If y'all will get one hundred acres of land, which we will have to approve, and give it to us, we will do it.'

"We looked all around and finally found the present site, twenty-eight acres belonging to the Smith family and behind was another eighty acres belonging to C. Agnew Thompson. The whole thing cost us sixty-four thousand dollars. We paid Thompson seven hundred dollars an acre for his and a lot of people raised Cain, saying it was outrageous. Actually, it was a pretty good deal.

"The college opened for business in 1964. We argued with the

State Board that some day we would have five hundred students. We used the Methodist church and the church of Christ for a meeting place for a year while the first three buildings were being built. They added other buildings one at a time and subsequently there were four thousand students.

"In the 1970 governor's campaign, George Wallace told me, 'Jimmy, if you want me to, I will make that a four-year college when I am elected.' I said, 'Thank you, governor.' He was elected and he appointed me to the Alabama Commission on Higher Education. I knew down in my heart that we did not need an additional four-year college, although I would like very much for us to have one here.

"I knew it was not in the state's best interest, and I told Governor Wallace. I told him it would cause him a lot of criticism and I would compromise with him if he would give us dormitories. That's the way we got dormitories, and that's the reason we were the only new junior college in the state to have dormitories," Faulkner recalls.

Bay Minette's new college was named William Lowndes Yancey State Junior College. At that time, it was customary to name these colleges after Southern patriots. Yancey was a Confederate leader and at the time the school was being organized Alabama, like other Southern states, was observing the centennial of the Confederacy.

But by the close of the sixties the climate had changed and in 1971 about thirty local citizens went to Montgomery and asked the State Board of Education to rename the school the James H. Faulkner Junior College. As the timing fell right after a hard-fought campaign for governor between Albert Brewer and George Wallace, the request needed the blessings of both men.

"A friend of mine went to [former] Governor Brewer to ask what he thought of it and he said, 'No! I don't want anything named for Jimmy Faulkner.' He had blamed me for his defeat. Then, he smiled and said, 'I am only joking. Jimmy Faulkner deserves it and I favor it.' Governor Wallace felt the same way, and the board voted nine to one to change the name. The lone dissenting vote was cast by the fellow who got the college for Monroeville. I guess he didn't like it because we got one.

"We've only had two presidents, Dr. Lathem Sibert and Dr. Gary Branch. People would ask me how Dr. Sibert got to be president of this college and I would say, 'I have no idea, except his wife was born in Clio, Alabama' [Governor Wallace's hometown].

"Naturally, I am honored to have the institution named for me. I am indebted to many people and I feel this obligation very deeply," Faulkner said.

Faulkner continues to work hard for the Baldwin County college named in his honor. He is chairman of the endowment fund and continues to raise money for the institution, including a campaign to raise several million dollars for new buildings and repair of existing structures. He says he stays out of the school's administration affairs but is interested in the college's progress.

"I toured South Carolina, North Carolina, and Virginia with the school's administrators studying systems that teach chefs and other culinary arts that we so badly need in this area. As a result of this, we were able to open a branch in Gulf Shores that has one of the best culinary schools in the nation. In fact, it won second in the nation for efficiency and quality in a 1999 contest," Faulkner boasts.

"I was also helpful and encouraged the opening of a branch in Fairhope, which has been very successful. Presently, I am trying to obtain funds and land to build dormitories at Gulf Shores so students from all over the country can come and learn culinary arts. It is easy for them to get jobs at the various restaurants and hotels in Gulf Shores, where they are always short of help," Faulkner adds.

With campuses in Gulf Shores, Fairhope and Bay Minette, all of Baldwin County's population of one hundred and fifty thousand is convenient to higher education. Up to four thousand take advantage of it each year. In its thirty-five years of successful operation, the number of alumni is fast approaching one million.

In 1977, Governor Wallace appointed Faulkner as a member of the Alabama Commission on Higher Education (ACHE).

"I was a great advocate of our two-year college system, as well as the universities, but most of the ACHE members did not look with favor on the two-year institutions. However, I kept fighting for them, and finally was made chairman of the Commission. I served in that position until 1985," Faulkner recalls.

"It was important to me to serve on ACHE because the commission has much to do with regulating higher education in Alabama. It recommends budgets for all the colleges and universities, both two-year and above, and it pretty much controls the number of courses in the two- year system, making sure no money is wasted on unnecessary duplication.

"I also realized that ACHE was under great influence from the four-year institutions and continually opposed the two-year schools, always claiming there were too many of them, not realizing that schools must not only be fine academically, they must be accessible," he contends.

Faulkner says that two-year schools furnish sixty-five percent of all freshmen today entering higher education in Alabama and that up to fifty percent of all Alabama's higher education students are in the two-year system. He contends that millions have attended these institutions since they were established more than thirty-five years ago. He says having affordable higher education available to every person in Alabama near home has not only saved the state tens of millions of dollars of education tax money but also has an economic impact on the state of about four billion dollars per year.

Faulkner uses an example close to home to back up his claim.

"The cost per student for the University of South Alabama is $7,092 while Baldwin County's community college is only $2,551. If you were to close all two-year schools in Alabama, and half of those students were to go to other higher education institutions, it would cost taxpayers the same. Sadly, at least fifty percent of the students could not go anywhere but would stay at home. This would be the most expensive alternative for the state, students not being educated," Faulkner adds.

"You hear it everywhere that Alabama has more two-year colleges than any surrounding state. Although we do have thirty-one two-year colleges, just look at nine other southeastern states. Arkansas has thirty-two, Florida has sixty-three, Georgia has forty-seven, Kentucky has thirty-seven, Louisiana has fifty, North Carolina has fifty-eight, Tennessee has forty, South Carolina has twenty-one, and Mississippi has fifteen.

"Education should be of high quality, but if it is not convenient and accessible to the student, it isn't of much value. Actually, more of our people, per capita, are going to colleges and universities in Alabama than all the other states in the nation, except North Dakota, Utah, and Kansas. This is something of which we all should be proud," Faulkner concludes.

Faulkner has received many awards and honors for his commitment to higher education including seven honorary doctorate degrees. He was conferred the official designation Alumnus Honoris Gratia "in grateful recognition of his many contributions and meritorious service to the university, the community and the state" by the University of Alabama, Birmingham, in 1982. Faulkner, along with Senator Howell Heflin, was the first to ever be so honored by UAB. Also in 1982, Faulkner received the Exemplary Dedication to Higher Education (EDHE) award by the Alabama Association of Colleges and Universities.

The greatest pleasure is in not what you do for yourself but what you do for God and others.

Jimmy Faulkner

15

A Centennial Man

I n January of 2000, the people of Bay Minette and Baldwin County sought to honor the "Person of the Century," a once-in-a-lifetime award for the person who had given most for their community and county during the past one hundred years. The difficult task was not determining the person honored, but rather how to adequately put into words a summary of a lifetime of achievements. The man was Jimmy Faulkner.

"For over six decades in our community, this man has been and remains today, an individual totally consumed with trying to improve the quality of life of his fellow man and the town, county, and state which he so dearly loves," proclaimed George Noonan who presented the award on behalf of the North Baldwin Chamber of Commerce.

"He remains the eternal optimist, a tireless promoter of our city and county at every opportunity and an encyclopedic source of information and history about almost every facet of Bay Minette's past, present, and future. His impact on the economic development of our community is legendary. Much of the economic activity and educational opportunity that we enjoy today in Bay

Minette and Baldwin County would be much different without the footprints and handprints of our honoree," Noonan added.

Faulkner's accomplishments are also recognized outside his home area. *Alabama Seaport* magazine, in its April 1999 edition, described the bounding octogenarian as "an Alabama icon . . . (who) keeps up with everything — and virtually everyone — in politics . . . having involved himself in hundreds of endeavors that have brought good to all of Alabama."

Business Alabama, in its February 1999 edition, described Faulkner as "a tireless worker for the county's industrial advancement . . . (who) has been successful through dogged persistence, energy in cultivating prospect interest and a style of avuncular indulgence in selling the interested party" in locating industries in Baldwin County.

In September 2000, Faulkner gained yet another honor. He received the "Ageless Hero" award for Alabama.

Sponsored by Blue Cross and Blue Shield, the award is given "in celebration of the spirit and vitality of our nation's seniors." Faulkner was nominated for the award by Congressman Sonny Callahan of Mobile for his outstanding achievements in the business and political arenas.

While most do not realize it, when he was in the state senate in the 1950s, Faulkner was even instrumental in passing legislation to move the Alabama-Florida state line along the coast more toward Florida, giving Baldwin County more sandy beach front which later was worth millions.

Faulkner is proud of his county. He points out that Baldwin became a county in 1809, making it ten years older than the state of Alabama, which did not become a state until 1819.

Baldwin County is now one of the most prosperous and fastest growing counties in Alabama. However, it was not always that way.

"When I came to the county in 1936, the only paved road was Highway 31 from Atmore to Stapleton, and from the Bay Minette courthouse to the railroad. There was no other pavement in the county anywhere, it was all dirt roads. And the money in the banks was less than a million dollars total deposits. And now, there must be at least three hundred million.

"When I came, the population of the entire county was a little over twenty-seven thousand. Now, there are more people in the Bay Minette area than there were in the whole county then," Faulkner remembers.

The fastest growing areas of the county continue to be around the Eastern Shore and the south area of Gulf Shores and Foley. Planners now predict that by 2020 everything south of Foley and west of Robertsdale up to Spanish Fort will all be urban.

"It's just amazing. There are fifteen thousand condominiums along the Gulf Coast of Baldwin County, and there are sixteen hundred more under construction now, and I know of at least another thousand being planned. Developers have about run out of places to build. It's unbelievable!" Faulkner exclaims.

Does Faulkner worry about too much progress and development in the area?

"No. To me, it's all good. It furnishes jobs for people and makes it a better place to live. Living conditions are better. We have happier lives, better schools, and everything. Now, it could get to the point that it might happen, but we're far away from it now," he adds.

Since arriving in Bay Minette in August of 1936, Faulkner has moved his office and business activities several times, but all within two hundred feet of each other and always in the shadow of the Baldwin County Courthouse. For more than fifty-three of those years, Dorothy Cooper Martin has been his able assistant who looked after business while Faulkner was busy away from the office.

"She is a very detail-oriented person and has kept me out of a lot of trouble. She is one of the most efficient secretaries and assistants anywhere," Faulkner boasts.

Although initially hired as a cashier, Mrs. Martin has held nearly every position in the newspaper business, was an officer in Faulkner's radio corporation, and in 1980 she was named secretary and treasurer of the Baldwin County Democratic Executive Committee when Faulkner resigned that post.

FAULKNER HAS DEVOTED his wholehearted efforts to improving the quality of life of all the citizens of his community and experienced great success in improving living conditions and education opportunities for African Americans.

In the early sixties, Faulkner worked through the Department of Housing and Urban Development to improve Bay Minette's substandard housing for minorities, an unusual feat for a small town to be included in a program generally utilized by major cities. It was not an easy task. Even after funding was approved, Faulkner had to visit suspicious individual residents to convince them to give up their slum dwellings for new housing that would be constructed.

Faulkner is known for treating all citizens with dignity and respect, providing every possible assistance, without regard to race or station in life. This fact is borne out in numerous examples, including that of a fifteen-year-old African American who began working after school as a janitor for Faulkner's Bay Minette radio station in the mid-fifties.

Bill Cox was only ten years old when his father was killed by an automobile. His mother was left to raise four children, three boys and a girl.

Bill worked at any odd jobs he could find to help in any way he could. He was delighted to land the janitorial job.

"I worked at the station, cleaning up the building, and I was hired by the station manager. It was some time later that I started working for the *Baldwin Times* and came in contact with Mr. Faulkner," Cox remembers.

"I just got connected to him. I was doing janitorial work at the paper, and then they started using me to work on getting the newspaper out on Wednesday nights. I remember that it was an all night job and I would stay until we took the paper to the post office the next morning. I did that for a number of years."

Faulkner, as he so often does to others, encouraged Cox to set higher goals and get a good education. The employer's advice apparently stuck.

"I was just always inspired, as well as fascinated by Mr. Faulkner. He just exuded confidence and professionalism as long as I have known him," Cox affirms.

After high school, Cox left Bay Minette and attended undergraduate school at Alabama A&M in Huntsville.

"My mother pretty much said that if you want to go to college, I will 'help' you. She never told me that she would send me. So I worked three-and-a-half years in work-study programs. I had really applied to only one college, and I was accepted there. I can't say that I had the motivation at the time, but once I got there, I knew I had to produce, and I did."

After graduation, he worked in Huntsville for four years before going to Europe. After six years in Europe, he returned to the states and lived in the Washington, D.C., area.

"There was a long disconnect between myself and Mr. Faulkner, with the exception of the times I would run into him in Bay Minette when I would go home to visit my mother and other relatives. We really didn't re-connect until I started my own business," Cox recalls.

Today, William E. Cox is the president and managing editor of *Black Issues in Higher Education* and other publications. It is no secret that his business holdings are worth millions. His business is headquartered in Washington, D.C.

"I also have an office in New York, and I live in a place called Clifton, Virginia, in Fairfax County. It's a little rural area, very quiet and away from the big lights. Actually, it reminds me of the rural areas near Bay Minette. You know, I like to have access to the city; I don't want to live there.

"Ironically, I ended up in the publishing field, which is almost parallel to a lot of the things that Mr. Faulkner has already done. For a number of years I even tried to acquire a broadcast property and I said, if that happens it is almost unbelievable. So I informed him that I was going to include him on my mailing list of publications, and then we started a dialogue, and we have been talking ever since."

Cox said that one of the biggest treats in his life was the day that Faulkner visited his Washington office.

"He was in the city and called me about 2:30 in the afternoon. He didn't have much time, only a couple of hours. I figured it would have taken me too long to drive down, bring him back, and return him to the airport, so I had a car to pick him up and bring him out to my office. I was able to show him around the complex, and that was a real treat for me, to sit down and have a cup of coffee and to introduce him to my own staff here. He's one of my favorite people.

"I know that he has always been inspired by the success that I have had, and I have always been inspired by his ability to be a leader, and to get things done.

"Sometimes there are people who, and in this case Mr. Faulkner, have served for many years as a mentor without knowing it. There are certain people that you just look up to, and that you respect. A person like him, he will always be 'Mr. Faulkner.' I can never see myself calling him 'Jimmy,' for example, regardless of how old I get. It's just that respect, if you will, and admiration you have for some people.

"And the thing about it, the man loves Bay Minette. The things I have noticed mostly is that he has always, as far as I know, been a very progressive person, trying to better the community, trying to bring industry to the community, trying to upgrade the standard of living for everybody living there . . . and I underline the word 'everybody,' because I saw him as an all inclusive individual, and not a selfish type person.

"Every time we talk, there is always an invitation to lunch or dinner, whether it is at a restaurant or at his home. And I have done the yard work at his house. But you know, I consider him a friend, with no strings. I know that he is very proud of me, and I am very proud of him," Cox affirms.

Cox, a distinguished man with graying mustache and dressed in a dark blue pin-striped suit, recently stepped quietly into a conference room of a major Washington, D.C., hotel. He sat on the back row as he proudly observed one of his employees, selected as one of three distinguished media panel members to advise university presidents attending the 2001 annual conference of the American Council on Education.

Cox is only one example of the many lives influenced by Faulkner. Faulkner has even encouraged his cook of twenty-seven years, Lula Lee, to continue her education and both are proud that she recently received her bachelor's degree in business.

Faulkner recently calculated that he has helped sixteen people who worked for him and became millionaires.

"Many of these worked as printers devils," he adds.

He smiles when he is reminded that he is often referred to as the ultimate "Southern Gentleman." At the same time, some considered him too liberal when he ran for governor.

"Although I had no strong feelings against the North, I was delighted to be a Southerner. I did feel the Yankees mistreated us and tried to make us suffer because of the Civil War, or War Between the States, which had been over for many years.

"They had such rules as Freight Rate Differentials which made people in the South pay more to ship things to the North than northerners paid to ship things to the South. That curtailed industrial development in our area. People like Senator Lister Hill and Governor Bibb Graves fought this and gradually changed the situation.

"I often jokingly say, 'I know Yankees are smarter than I am, but I do not like for them to tell me so.'

"I still feel, as a general rule, that people who come from north of the Mason-Dixon Line feel somewhat superior to us. Having gone to school in the Midwest, the University of Missouri, when I returned home I was accused of not having a Southern brogue, and I resented this. I was proud of my Southern upbringing and speech."

Does Faulkner feel that he had a greater acceptance for integration than most Southerners of his time?

"Yes, and it reflected against me when I ran for office. However, I think that I was right, and that time and circumstances have so proven.

"We should all be on equal terms. We must realize that we all can be successful if only we are honest, hard working, intelligent, and have a good attitude. Too many people think they fail because of racism.

"The citizens of the United States have never had the opportunities for success as they have today. Fortunately, many are taking advantage of it while others continue to have the wrong attitude."

Boaz commanded his young men, saying, Let her glean even among the sheaves, and reproach her not; And let fall also some of the handfuls of purpose for her, and leave them, that she may glean them, and rebuke her not.

Ruth 2:15-16

16

Gleaning "Handfuls on Purpose"

I n the Old Testament, we learn that it was a custom to allow those less fortunate to glean the grain fields behind the harvesters so that they might have small amounts of grain for food. The mighty Boaz spotted Ruth, a foreigner, among the gleaners in his field and asked his servants who she was. When told that this woman was a damsel from Moab, Boaz had compassion and not only allowed her to continue gleaning, but directed his servants to leave some grain on purpose for her.

After gleaning the information for the preceding chapters of this book, there remained certain "handfuls" that may best be described as miscellany, but are nonetheless as important as other information previously harvested. This potpourri is contained, in no special order, in this chapter.

Heritage

For years the Faulkners of Alabama had believed that their family came from Virginia and North Carolina. However, with the popularity of computers, Jimmy Faulkner's first cousin, Elaine

Hartley Winger, believed she had traced the family back to a James Faulkner in England.

"When my grandfather died, he wanted me to have the family Bible, and there were two or three handwritten pages from one of those nickel tablets that we used to take to school. We don't know who wrote the note, but it said there were three brothers who came South from the Virginia and North Carolina areas. One stopped in Lamar County; his name was Burrell, who was my great-grandfather. He was the first probate judge of Lamar County. Another went to Arkansas, and they never did know where the third one went. We assumed he went to Mississippi, but no one has ever been able to connect him with William Faulkner in that group," Faulkner remembers.

"My Great-Grandpa spelled his name 'Falkner,' the theory being that probate judges did everything by writing, so he just cut the 'u' out so that he could write a little faster. But my mother put the 'u' back in because everybody in Lamar County would mispronounce it. And on my father and mother's tombstone it's spelled 'Falkner' because the man at the Columbus, Mississippi, marble works didn't ask anybody, but just assumed that, because my grandfather's name was spelled 'Falkner,' but we never said anything about it because it doesn't matter."

Faulkner's grandmother was Alabama Jane Hays, daughter of Andrew Jackson Hays who, in 1824, was the first of their family to be born in Alabama.

On Longevity

Jimmy Faulkner comes from a family of long-living people. His father's youngest sister died at the age of ninety-four. Faulkner's great-uncle, Burrell Faulkner, died at the age of one hundred and three.

"My desire is to outlive the age of Uncle Burrell," Faulkner smiles.

"When he was one hundred years old, his friends and neighbors decided to give him a celebration, so we all met at Lamar County High School auditorium. Senator Jim Allen was the speaker who introduced him and presented him a plaque.

"Uncle Burrell, a small but feisty man, jumped up, accepted the plaque, and then said, 'Thank you for this honor, but I do not make speeches. When I was a young boy I went up in the hills behind the house to practice a speech. I practiced it under a chestnut tree . . . the tree died.'

"Then he sat down without saying another word," Faulkner recalls.

Faulkner says there are advantages and disadvantages of reaching old age.

"Obviously, it is better than any alternative, unless you are a suffering invalid. Of course, you lose some of your physical and mental faculties, but generally speaking, if you are in good health you will do fine.

"Of course, another disadvantage is that you lose a lot of long-time friends who can never be replaced. Also, as one gets older one is prone to be more pessimistic. This should be avoided because without optimism, nothing great can be accomplished."

"People often tell me they don't understand how I can have so much energy at my age. Actually, sometimes I feel that I am lazy. But I have always maintained that when I go to bed at night, I want to know that during the day I have done something good for someone, either an individual, my family, my community, my state or my country."

A Coronary Event

In 1985, Faulkner's longevity was threatened by a problem with his heart. He and his doctor discovered the symptom during a scheduled visit to his cardiologist.

"I was taking a stress test and the doctor stopped the machine. He said, 'I want you to have another test.'

"I said, 'In about two weeks or so?'

"And he said, 'How about tomorrow?'"

Although confronted with the news that he must have open-heart surgery, Faulkner did not believe that his life was in danger.

"I didn't think I was going to die. They operated on me as quickly as they could get the doctor, which happened to be a couple of days. I didn't have any trouble, except it was very painful," Faulkner added.

In fact, Faulkner's friends observed that the operation seemed to be a blessing, and that Faulkner, after recovery, actually had more drive and energy than before the surgery.

"I have been very fortunate since. I take exercises and try to do everything my doctor tells me. For example, I exercise my back about fifteen minutes, then I get onto the treadmill machine for about twenty minutes to get my heart rate up to a hundred and five, and keep it there for awhile.

"I used to walk three miles a day with my golden retriever, but Missy died. Now I save time by getting on the machine. I don't run because it jars me. My goal is to get two hundred minutes of exercise a week. I try to do my exercise, get dressed, and get into the office by nine o'clock."

War On Terrorism

As one who remembers well the attack on Pearl Harbor, and

also the more recent terrorist attack on the United States September 11, 2001, how would Faulkner compare the two?

"Well, there was a faster solidification of morale and patriotism in the terrorist attack. In Pearl Harbor, it was thousands of miles away and we really did not realize the significance of it until President Roosevelt made his 'Day of Infamy' speech.

"Of course, we did not have television back in 1941 to see what was actually happening. We did not see it that same day. In the terrorist attack in New York City, television was on the scene and we saw first-hand what was happening, the horror of the airplanes crashing into the twin towers. It had an immediate and lasting effect on all of us.

"In the case of Pearl Harbor, we knew, of course, what the Japanese wanted to do. It was quite evident that they wanted to destroy us by first destroying the Pacific Fleet. They had a country, they had a flag, and they had a military force.

"The terrorists also wanted to destroy us but, in this case, it was not clear who our enemy was or where they were located. They were secretive, dug into holes in the mountains, requiring a different kind of war than from World War II.

"In this war, there are no beachheads, no national borders of attack, and no conventional military operations. We have to employ various methods of finding the enemy, cutting off military supplies and their financial support."

Returning Telephone Calls

Jimmy Faulkner is known for his meticulous detail in returning telephone calls.

"Although I try to get into the office by nine, the time I arrive depends largely on the number of phone calls I receive before leaving the house. Anyone calling my office before I arrive there is transferred to my home. I learned a long time ago, you save a lot of time if you take calls when they come in rather than having to return them.

"I also refuse to let my staff ask who is calling because I talk to all my callers as quickly as possible.

"If you have as many as five or six calls during the day that you have not answered, or have not responded to when they call, you could spend several hours trying to make contact with people. Besides, then you have to pay the expense of the call if it is long distance," Faulkner noted.

Since his heart surgery, Faulkner tries to obey his doctor's advice and take a brief nap after lunch.

"If at home, I eat lunch at noon, read the newspapers for about fifteen minutes and try to take a nap from thirty to forty-five minutes. I return to the office after the nap, although I usually get at least two calls during the nap."

Key to Success

Faulkner believes that the success of any business depends on the attention to detail. Although he claims he is not too good at details, he has always been lucky and smart enough to employ people around him who take care of such matters.

"What success I have enjoyed was caused by my sincere love of people, friendliness and being willing to take conservative and moderate risks, which I did numerous times. Some of these turned out to be more risky than anticipated, but usually I pulled through.

"Never having much cash, I never really played it close to the chest but I took risks that most people probably would not have taken. I never objected to borrowing money if I could make an investment I felt reasonably sure would make it possible for me to repay it. My decisions were usually the right ones.

"However, one of my weaknesses was that I too often tried to help people in need. I have lost considerable money trying to help people, some of whom turned out to be successful, but others became ingrates, were unsuccessful, and cost me a lot of money.

"Still, my philosophy is that if and when I get to the point that I can't help my fellow man and the Lord, I have no further need to be around."

Ingratitude — Greatest Sin

> Blow, blow, thou winter wind!
> Thou art not so unkind as man's ingratitude.
> > Shakespeare

On the wall of Faulkner's office is a framed saying which states, "I cannot tell you how to succeed, but I can tell you how to fail. Try to please everybody."

During the course of his long, successful career Faulkner has made many friends, but also some enemies.

"You like to have everybody as a friend, but you've got to make decisions sometimes. And they say that every ball hit makes somebody happy, and somebody unhappy. And I've hit a lot of balls. And a lot of people criticize me, and you know, I don't know why on earth they do.

"A person who I had helped several times came in to my office one day and railed me out. The fact that I had previously helped did not seem to matter. This person just didn't like something that I had done, or some way that I had looked. So not everybody likes you."

Faulkner's friends say the reason is jealousy.

Faulkner can list numerous examples of people whom he has helped who, in turn, proved to be ingrates or even enemies.

Is this a part of being involved politically?

"Well, you have to accept it. I don't like it, but I accept it. And if any of them come back and want me to help them, I try to help them. I've changed a lot of people. I have had a lot of people come in and say, 'Well, Mr. Faulkner, I just had the wrong idea about you. I just didn't know.'

"So you try to overcome those things by being humble. Humility is very inexpensive and very profitable. But it seems that when you do things for some people, they don't appreciate it, but may even resent it.

"Dr. Ralph Adams once told me that Julius Caesar said that the greatest sin is that of ingratitude. When you do something for somebody, you don't expect them to come up and thank you, and make all over you, and all of that, but you do expect them not to resent it or stab you in the back.

"I've learned this too. A person who shows ingratitude, if he does it once, he'll do it again if he thinks it's to his advantage. It is the one trait of people that cannot be corrected. If you catch someone lying, you can correct that. If you catch them stealing, that can be corrected. But ingratitude is something that people never seem to overcome. Maybe I'm wrong on that, but that's been my observation.

"However most people are appreciative and return in kind when they have the opportunity. It flatters me to know how many loyal friends I do have."

Just Whistlin'

Jimmy Faulkner was born into a hard-working, Christian family who enjoyed the simple pleasures of life. It was not until after his father died and the family moved to Vernon that he saw his first motion picture.

"They had no theaters there, but the first movie I ever saw was in a high school auditorium. Some traveling person came through and rented the place to show us Harold Lloyd. He was a great comedian and we enjoyed it very much. Of course, these were silent movies.

"As we got a little older, around thirteen or fourteen, there was a fellow in Vernon who rented a store and showed movies once or twice a week. They were mostly westerns, which I thoroughly enjoyed. The first talking movie I ever saw was in Columbus, Mississippi, and it was Al Jolson in 'Sonny Boy,'" Faulkner recalled.

During the early boyhood years on the farm, Faulkner was taught to enjoy work, made easier by singing and whistling.

"I was almost always whistling doing whatever job I had to do, if whistling did not disturb others. I would whistle and I would sing. I was always singing when I was plowing or hoeing. We used to joke, saying, I could plow and sing all four parts of a song.

"But even my daddy would whistle, and my brother would whistle, too. Maybe not a tune, but they would whistle," Faulkner said.

What has happened to the art of whistling today?

"I just don't know. You never hear anybody whistling anymore. Have you ever thought about that? I have wondered about it. I don't know how long it's been since I've heard somebody just whistle. I guess they've gotten too busy, or they have television to watch. I guess we just had to whistle and do things like that to entertain ourselves back then," Faulkner concluded.

Sadly, perhaps cell phones and television have replaced the joyful singing and whistling of the past.

Chinese "Daughters"

Jimmy Faulkner's travels have taken him to many places and

have led to many lasting associations. However, no trip has been more meaningful than one taken to Hong Kong in 1983.

During that visit Faulkner met George Liu, a prominent attorney, and the two became great friends. Liu visited Faulkner in Alabama several times.

"George told me that he had a good friend in China who was a high government official but made only three hundred dollars a month. He said the man had two daughters that he was anxious to have educated in America, but could not financially afford it. I told him that if he would handle the legal matters in getting them to the United States, we would 'adopt' them and pay for their education," Faulkner said.

"Wang Yin, the oldest, arrived in 1984 and entered school that fall at Faulkner University in Montgomery. She had not started school in China until she was twelve because she had been diagnosed with a disease and they thought she would not live long. Later she was diagnosed with arthritis.

"Soon after entering college here, the arthritis affected her so badly she could hardly get out of bed. We sent her to the University of Alabama Hospital in Birmingham where they operated on both hips and both knees.

"She was in Birmingham a while when her younger sister, Wang Yi, came to Bay Minette. She was a very attractive young lady and I told Evelyn that Wang Yi was so beautiful she'd never get back to China.

"Both went to college and graduated cum laude. Wang Yin continued her education and got her degree in law, while Wang Yi became an accountant. Both now live in Houston and Wang Yi is now Mrs. Jason Shi, with two fine daughters. Wang Yin is practicing law and has been successful.

"While living in our home, they were an inspiration and worked hard learning English. They had a smattering of English when they arrived, as English is the second language Chinese learn in school."

Family

Traditions are important in the Faulkner family. Faulkner believes in staying in touch with all the family members on a regular basis, and holidays are special treats.

"We have two sons and their lovely wives, eight grandchildren and eleven great-grandchildren. We get together often with all or part of the family. We always get as many of the family together as possible at Christmas time. We exchange presents, eat a lot of turkey and other good food and have a good time catching up on each other's activities. It is fun staying in touch with them and learning of their achievements, problems, and about their children. We are very fortunate in that all of our family is now located in Montgomery, Selma, Mobile, and Bay Minette—none out of Alabama."

One of Faulkner's granddaughters, Mary Jane Harris, who lives with her husband, Floyd, in Lanett, near the Alabama-Georgia line, remembers fondly the special holidays, and her childhood association with her grandfather.

"Last year, everybody was there for Christmas dinner but two. We had a total of twenty-eight there, and we had our pictures made in front of Grandpa's house. We had a big Christmas dinner with turkey, dressing, ham, sweet potatoes, and all the trimmings of a traditional Christmas meal. We sat around and talked, and the great-grandkids played," she said.

How long has this tradition been going on?

"I can't remember not having it. It's always been that way. Uncle Wade's family and my daddy's family have always had Christmas there, and we get together at other times, too," she added.

Mary Jane especially treasures the childhood memories of the times together at the home of her grandparents.

"I remember always wanting to spend the night with them when I was growing up. When I was about eight years old, I would ask Mother, 'Let me spend the night with Grandpa and Grandma?' She would say, 'Well, did they call and invite you?' I would say, 'No,' and then I would run upstairs and call Grandpa and say, 'Grandpa, call me back and ask me to spend the night.' About five minutes later, the phone would ring and it would be Grandpa inviting me to spend the night. I finally got smart and didn't even ask my mother. I would just call Grandpa and say, 'Grandpa, how about calling and see if I can spend the night tonight?'"

What was so special about spending the night across town at her grandparents' home?

"Well, they had lots of candy. They had a trampoline, a pool table downstairs, they had a huge yard and all the neighborhood kids would get together and play hide-and-seek in their yard. It was just a lot of fun," she said, "and I remember going on walks with Grandpa."

Was her grandfather a strict disciplinarian?

"Well, he didn't hesitate to get on to us. He never spanked us or anything like that, but he would tell us how disappointed he was about something that we did, and that was sometimes worse than a spanking," she smiled.

Mary Jane remembers that her grandfather also stayed in touch with her after her childhood days.

"When I was away at boarding school in Vicksburg, Mississippi, and when I was in college in Montgomery, he would fly to see me. On long weekends, he would send his plane to pick me up and take me home. I remember that I would always get excited when he would come to visit me in Montgomery and someone from the office would tell me that my grandaddy was there."

Mary Jane considers Faulkner more than a grandfather, he is also a close friend.

"Anytime that I have ever had a problem, I felt like I could call him and talk with him about it. I think I talk to Grandaddy about two times a week. He usually calls me late at night and asks me what I'm doing. I appreciate Grandpa keeping after me. I was thirty when I graduated from college, and he never slacked off on me about that. Constantly he would say, 'You can do it. You know you can!' And now, he's on me about working on my master's, and I know it's the right thing to do."

She thinks of her grandfather as a man of faith, a "very religious" person who wants to help others.

"I think he would do anything in the world to help somebody. I remember when I was working for the power company I had a friend that I felt sorry for. She never had the chance to go to college. She had lived in an orphanage. She acted like she wanted to go several times. I called Grandpa and he sent me the money, and we bought her the books and everything. Well, she went for about three or four days and dropped out. She didn't have the receipts to take the books back, or anything. I thought Grandpa might get upset with me about that, but he never said anything about it," she remembers.

"I can't imagine what life would be without him," Mary Jane concluded.

Faulkner's other grandchildren, Henry Wade Faulkner, Jr., Jim Faulkner, III, Jenny Camp, Beth Taupeka, twins Rebecca Stewart and Rachel Todd, and Jay Faulkner, would tell you similar things about their Grandpa.

How would Faulkner like to be remembered?

"The only thing that has always interested me is to live and do in such a way as to make my family proud of me, now and for as long as they live.

"I feel that so far as the community, the church, and the world remembers me is not of great importance, unless it is in a negative way, which I trust will not be the case. I have been engaged in many activities for the benefit of my community, church, family, and wider areas. Naturally, it would be nice if I was remembered and appreciated for this fact. However, I am fully aware that good things you may have done in the past won't last, as the general philosophy of man is, 'What have you done for me lately,'" Faulkner concludes.

His family would agree that a part of Faulkner's greatness has come from the fact that, throughout his life, he always has left behind those "handfuls on purpose" for those in need.

Building Bay Minette & Baldwin County

J immy Faulkner believes that sometimes good things happen, but not often. If they are worthwhile, somebody has worked hard to make things happen.

If there are two words that describe Faulkner's approach to recruiting industry and other civic projects for his community, those words are "persistence" and "optimism." Faulkner is an eternal optimist with the persistence of a pitbull.

Faulkner emphasizes that no one person accomplishes anything worthwhile alone. In all of his efforts, he had the cooperation of city, county, and state government officials as well as local citizens.

In August of 1940, at age twenty-four, Faulkner became mayor of Bay Minette.

On the city council were five men twice his age. They were bank president Emanuel E. Davidson, nursery owner O. J. Manci, County Engineer E. N. Rodgers, hardware store co-owner L. D. Owen, and drugstore owner J. H. Stacey. Faulkner believes that as a group, it was as fine a business-oriented council that the city has ever had.

J. B. Blackburn was attorney and J. L. Barrow was police chief, street maintenance superintendent, and most everything else pertaining to the city's physical properties. The city owned no utilities. Natalie Feulner was town clerk when Faulkner took office and, after her resignation, she was succeeded by Mary Smith.

The city's annual budget was slightly over twelve thousand dollars with revenue coming in almost equally from ad valorem taxes, business licenses, and fines. The mayor's salary was one hundred dollars every three months.

"I served until March of 1943 when I resigned to enter the U.S. Army Air Corps as an aviation cadet," Faulkner remembers.

"In the meantime, I was editor and publisher of the *Baldwin Times,* served on the U. S. War Savings Bond staff for the state of Alabama, and became president of the Alabama Press Association.

"The population was only about fourteen hundred and our crime rate was not high. I don't think we had any crime. The worst things were some drinking, crap shooting, and such other minor things."

Faulkner remembers three important things that happened during his time as mayor.

"A few months after I took office we were able to pay the last fifteen hundred dollars of a debt incurred paving Hand Avenue from the courthouse to Railroad Street. I gave my predecessor, J. C. Burns, credit for his frugality and good business practices for getting the city in good financial shape.

"With the consent of the council, I arranged to buy the water system from the Alabama Water Service Company for seventy-five thousand dollars to be paid over a few years at one and a half percent interest. The deal was not closed until after I had gone into the Air Corps. Upon my return home after obtaining my pilot wings in December of 1943, I found that the council had paid one hundred fifty thousand and agreed to pay three percent interest for something that had already been agreed upon. I hit the ceiling! However, the deal had already been made except Frank Holmes, president of the Baldwin County Bank, did intercede and agreed to finance the transaction at one and a half percent, thus saving considerable money. Until we bought the system, we had ten fire hydrants for which we had to pay ten dollars per month. This was quite a drag on our meager funds and I did talk them into giving us twelve hydrants without any cost.

"The most important thing I did as mayor was to persuade the council to put in a natural gas system for the city. In 1941, Ray R. Litrell of Florida came to see me, proposing to build the gas system for the city. After a survey was conducted, he said that we could sign up one hundred and fifty customers in the beginning. A few of the council, principally E. N. Rodgers, an accomplished engineer, loudly stated that this would never happen. Others were doubtful but we did go ahead and let a contract, two weeks before Pearl Harbor, for forty-eight thousand dollars to run a three-inch line, the biggest pipe obtainable at the time, from the edge of the city on Highway 31 South, to service the town. Since this was the first city-owned natural gas system in Alabama, we could not get the financing. Mr. Litrell begged me to go in with him on a fifty percent basis and we would buy the system, which I knew would be a good moneymaker. However, I told him it would be a conflict of interest, since I was mayor, and I would not do so. He finally agreed to finance it for fifty thousand dollars.

"The gas system was a lifesaver during the war and additional gas made it possible to keep Newport Industries here several years and it became the city's biggest gas user. The system gained additional business customers, along with several thousand homeowners. In almost sixty years this system has produced millions of dollars in profits for the city of Bay Minette, thus easing the tax burden on most citizens, besides the comfort of having natural gas in homes, and to attract industries," Faulkner maintains.

Working for More Industries and New Jobs

When Faulkner returned from the Army Air Corps as a pilot in 1945, the city had organized a Chamber of Commerce, which had only been in operation a few months. The president was Emanuel Davidson, local businessman, successful turpentine operator and landowner.

"Upon my arrival, Davidson told me that they saved a special spot for me on the Chamber and that I was selected to be chairman of the Industrial Development Committee, a position I still hold.

"In the meantime, I helped organize the Industrial Development Board of the city of Bay Minette in the early sixties and was chairman until recently. Also, we organized a corporation we called Bay Minette Mills, Incorporated, for the purpose of attracting industry. It was a simple Alabama tax-paying corporation, but through it we were able to help some industries locate in Bay Minette.

"During this time Bay Minette probably has been more successful than most towns our size in getting new industries, but perhaps not as successful as our reputation outside the town would indicate. Some other towns got larger industries, perhaps, but we are well diversified with some thirty-five industries obtained over the years with about thirty-five hundred employees.

"The opening of every industry in Bay Minette has an interesting story."

The stories are told, primarily in Faulkner's own words, of many of these adventures.

International Paper Company Container Division

It was about 5 o'clock in the afternoon in 1964 when two gentlemen entered the *Baldwin Times* office. One was George Wurtele, L & N Railroad's general manager for industrial development, from Jacksonville, Florida. The other was a mystery man.

"I had known George and he told me he would not give me the name of the gentleman with him, just simply stating that he was looking for an industrial site in Georgia. Since they had been unable to find a suitable place, they had come down through Pensacola up the Fort Morgan branch of the L & N Railroad from Foley and were tired.

"The project was so secretive that his friend did not want to come into the newspaper office with George, but George persuaded him that I was chairman of the industrial board and would keep everything confidential," Faulkner remembers.

"Naturally, being interested, I invited them to go a few miles out of town to Malbis to eat dinner. At that time Malbis was one of the finest restaurants in the area.

"Before the night was over, I not only knew the gentleman's name was Bob Hazelwood, but that he was representing the Container Division of International Paper Company out of the New York office, who was looking for a site.

"Explaining to me their needs, he said they had to have a twenty-acre site with a railroad in the rear and with a four-lane highway in front, and admitted there weren't many such sites.

"I showed him the twenty-acre site on Highway 31 South that belonged to G. K. Page and told him that possibly he might sell it. Finally, after weeks of negotiations, International Paper agreed that if we could obtain the land they would be interested in putting their plant here. They agreed to pay a thousand dollars per acre for the land but there was a strip right on the highway Page did not own which had three small rental houses that belonged to Devan Stapleton. After more weeks of negotiation, these houses and the two acres of land were purchased and the company was ready to go.

"However, John Patterson was the governor and a local friend, C. Lenoir Thompson, persuaded Patterson and the highway department to move Highway 31 from the west where it was to go around Bay Minette, to turn to the east, crossing two railroads and splitting this twenty-acre site wide open. This killed the project.

"Not long after, George C. Wallace was elected governor and he and his highway director agreed to keep the highway in its present location. However, the road was not four-laned but we assured International Paper that we would get it done as soon as possible.

"Seemingly all set to go again, the company sent a cablegram through their Mobile International Company headquarters and the vice president read it. He then ran a big story in the *Mobile Press Register,* stating that International Paper had agreed to build a container division plant at a cost of two million dollars inside the fence at the paper company in Mobile. He misinterpreted the message because it said that it would be built 'on land owned by the company outside Mobile.'

"The paper mill was on land inside the city limits of Mobile.

"Not wanting to embarrass the vice president, the plant was delayed again, in fact for so long, we thought it might never be built. But a few months later they called from New York stating that they were ready to go and sent people down to talk about the project.

"To make sure everything was all right, I had to take them to Montgomery to talk to the governor and the highway director, Guerry Pruitt, to make sure Highway 31 was not going to interfere with them. This was done, but before we could get started, another hitch came. The New York office called me and stated their attorney had just discovered they did not own the mineral rights under the twenty acres and that International Paper never built anything on any site on which they did not own the mineral rights. I tried to explain to them that there was no coal in the area and the only possible interference might be oil, but they stated again, emphatically, mineral rights or no building.

"Desperately, I wondered where on earth I could buy back the mineral rights. I finally thought of a possible solution. I asked city attorney J. B. Blackburn to search the records and he discovered that the mineral rights were sold by Dr. Walter B. Jones, retired state geologist and a real estate person in Huntsville. I knew Dr. Jones and I called him to explain our situation. I told him the plant would employ a hundred and fifty people, and this was very important to Bay Minette, even though it might not be important in Huntsville. He was friendly but gave me no solution.

"Fortunately, the next day he called me and said, 'Jimmy, if you can find twenty acres within a mile south or southeast of the property, I will get the man who bought the rights, who is now in Europe, to swap with you.'

"Still not knowing where I could find the twenty acres, a thought occurred to me. We had just finished a drive to raise $173,000 to upgrade the pants factory and buy one hundred acres of land to build a junior college that the state board of education and Governor Wallace had promised to put here.

"The one hundred acres of junior college land was still in the name of the Bay Minette Industrial Board. Well, when it was later transferred to the state department of education, they got one hundred acres of land but only eighty acres of mineral rights.

"Two guesses where the other twenty went," Faulkner smiles.

International Paper was now ready to begin construction, and the plant was dedicated in March 1966.

Faulkner, as chairman of the industrial board, was slated to welcome International Paper to Bay Minette. He had just acquired new bifocal glasses and was strolling happily into his *Times* office when he stumbled on the curb and fell, injuring his head. The concussion landed him into the local Mattie L. Rhodes Hospital for the night and State Representative L. D. "Dick" Owen then took over the honors of welcoming the new plant to the city.

After the ceremony, company officials paid a hospital visit to Faulkner to thank him for his efforts in helping them.

Faulkner also recalls another interesting incident related to International Paper.

"The state highway department appropriated money to four-lane Greeno Road in Fairhope, but the mayor of the town at that time refused the money as he did not want the road widened. You can guess who jumped on the situation, and we got four lanes, and thus the front of the International Paper had a four-lane highway and all our commitments were met.

"During all of this, they had to have enough water pressure to put in a sprinkler system in their building. Harry Still, Sr., manager of the Bay Minette utilities, and the city officials agreed to spend over three hundred thousand dollars to build a million-gallon water tank on an acre of land that was deeded to them from the plant.

"After thirty-five years of operation the plant is still going well. And after expenditures of over ten million dollars at various times, they have given permanent employment to around a hundred and fifty people with good wages."

Kaiser Aluminum

In the spring of 1963, the former mayor and postmaster of Birmingham, Cooper Green, who at the time was the vice president in charge of industrial development for Alabama Power Company, contacted Faulkner. Green said that Kaiser Aluminum was interested in obtaining eight acres of land on a railroad near Mobile.

"He told me that he and the Mobile Chamber of Commerce had spent several months persuading the company to locate in this area and, since after that decision was made, it was up to the local communities to persuade them to locate within their city.

"We welcomed the chance and showed them what acres of land belonged to Bay Minette Land Company on the Fort Morgan Branch of L & N Railroad just south of town and just off Highway 31. It was a beautiful site and they said they only needed eight acres on which they wanted to erect a plant to produce aluminum wire.

"In the meantime, I was negotiating with the land company to purchase the land and they had verbally agreed to sell us the forty acres at three hundred dollars per acre, but we had not received the deed. Kaiser was anxious and I told them we had the land, and they said they were coming here the following Monday to make the announcement and groundbreaking. Fine, but we did not yet have the deed.

"Naturally, I spent a pretty sleepless weekend. But as luck would have it, we got the deed through the mail on that Monday morning. All went well. However, when they found out that we were going to let them have eight acres for three hundred an acre they then decided they wanted the entire forty acres. We agreed, provided they would expand and put more buildings on it, which they agreed but never did.

"The plant opened later and ultimately employed about a hundred high paid people making their payroll the highest in Bay Minette, although not the biggest employment by numbers.

"One time they needed to employ three people and they had over three thousand applicants.

"Kaiser was delighted with the operation and the president of the company, Cornell Maier out of Oakland, California, had a Kaiser board meeting here so he could show them the Bay Minette plant. He stated that when he retired he was going to come here and manage it.

"The Kaiser connection was a happy one and I made two or three trips to their Oakland headquarters trying to get them to expand. They also expressed interest in putting in an aluminum smelter on the Tensaw River.

"However, after operating from 1965 to 1987, they had to close the plant because of worldwide competition, mainly out of Russia. Even though they were well pleased with their operations here, they closed all of their aluminum wire plants throughout the nation.

"As with other industrial development we had complete cooperation of the industrial board, as well as the city and county officials. It takes a community working together to be successful in industrial development. One person may be a leader, but everybody must cooperate," Faulkner maintains.

Alpine Industries Laboratories

On one occasion Faulkner had to become personally involved financially in locating an industry for his hometown.

"In mid-1976, Jack Boykin was considering putting in a chemical plant somewhere in the Mississippi or Alabama area.

"A native of Talladega County, Alabama, and a graduate of Georgia Tech in chemical engineering, he was an expert in the field of chemistry manufacturing. He wanted to manufacture intermediate organic chemicals in a plant that would cost about two million dollars.

"Fortunately, my two sons and I owned about twenty acres of land at Carpenter's Station on the railroad and he liked the site, but like so many industrial prospects, he did not have the money. Finally, I agreed to endorse a note and we borrowed two million from Farmers Home Administration through the First National Bank of Mobile. For the first time, I became a partner in an industrial plant.

"Although never employing many people—usually around five or six—the plant did well and after a few years of operation we decided to sell to Uniroyal, a big company in tires, chemicals and other things, for a nice profit.

"Uniroyal is still operating successfully on the site but has never employed more than four or five people. However, it is a fine addition to the Bay Minette industrial community."

Baldwin Utility Structures

Faulkner maintains that Bay Minette has always struggled hard to attract outside industries, but he is even more delighted when local people decide to invest in manufacturing plants to produce jobs.

"That was the case in 1989 when two local successful business-men, Tom McMillan and Tom Mitchell, proposed to build a plant, Baldwin Utility Structures, to manufacture, sell, and distribute concrete utility poles.

"The Industrial Development Board of the city of Bay Minette proposed to ask for a two million dollar bond allocation from the State Industrial Development Authority for permission to grant the bond issue. The plant was to employ in the neighborhood of twenty-five to thirty people and expected to begin operation about the middle of 1990.

"After several years of successful operation the plant was sold to Sherman Utility Structures, a German company, that owned a plant in Tuscaloosa and other places.

"An interesting incident happened to the local plant before the sale. About 60 percent of their production was to the Southern Company. Being a parent company of Alabama Power Company, they decided to consolidate all of their purchases of concrete poles from one source, which was Sherman.

"Tom McMillan approached me about the proposal and frankly admitted that without the power company's business, they would have to cut down to a very small operation and might not be able to continue at all.

"I called Elmer Harris, president of Alabama Power Company, and told him what would happen to our plant here in Bay Minette if they consolidated all of their purchases to Sherman. The order had already gone out from Atlanta headquarters to start purchasing from Sherman, but Mr. Harris stopped this and Baldwin Utility Structures continued to get business.

"However, a few months later, McMillan called me and stated that I was going to be mad at him because they agreed to sell their plant to Sherman. Of course, I was not mad and was, in fact, glad that I was able to help the two local owners get considerably more money for their plant since they continued to have the power company business.

"When Sherman purchased the plant in July of 1996, the employment was forty-two people. The plant continues to operate successfully."

Baldwin Lighting

Faulkner would soon have another pleasant experience with the two local businessmen regarding industry.

"After several months, Tom McMillan and Tom Mitchell decided to put in another concrete pole plant for the purpose of making smaller poles for lighting tennis courts, athletic fields, and such.

"Although their business has never grown real large, they have enjoyed a good, profitable operation.

"Baldwin Lighting purchased twelve acres of land on White Avenue, which belonged to the Bay Minette Industrial Board, at a reasonable price. The board had bought the land several years before for a thousand dollars per acre," Faulkner said.

Eastwood-Neally Company

Faulkner has learned that it usually takes a lot of hard work and long persuasion periods to get a new plant to locate. However, this was not the case with Eastwood-Nealley Company, a Belleville, New Jersey, firm.

"In September of 1967, I was out of town and Mrs. Martin, my longtime executive secretary, received a call from two gentlemen wanting to come to Bay Minette to see about locating an industry here. Immediately, she got in touch with me.

"At the time, we did not have a good motel in Bay Minette so I invited the two gentlemen to spend the night in our home at 705 East Fifth Street. They arrived the following Monday and were shown prospective industrial sites, as well as the Standard Furniture Manufacturing Company which had just rebuilt a thirty-thousand-square-foot building following a fire in 1959.

"We went out to eat that night. After spending the night with us, the next morning, following breakfast, they said they wanted to see the site on West Seventh Street. We went back to the nineteen-acre site toward the airport and they wanted to know if it was available and how much it would cost.

"Knowing that the Baldwin County Bank owned the land, I called Emanuel Davidson, the president, and told him of the interests of the company and asked if we could get an option on the land for a few days. He suggested the price of two thousand dollars an acre, and I talked him into making it a thousand per acre since it would be for a new plant, employing local people. He agreed.

"I asked him how long it would take to get an option and he said he could get it by Thursday. I stated that this was too long, knowing that all he would have to do was to go talk with another board member and the attorney for the bank, J. B. Blackburn, and they could agree if they wanted to. In a few minutes he called back and said they could have an option for one thousand an acre.

"After receiving the option, they left. I later learned they went to Oxford, Mississippi, where they already owned a site, planning to put their plant there.

"After disappointing the Oxford people by telling them they were not going to locate there, they went on to Memphis, Tennessee.

"The two gentlemen called me on a Wednesday from Memphis and Mrs. Martin found me in the lobby of the Jefferson Davis Hotel in Montgomery. Talking to them on the phone, they said they had decided to put the plant in Bay Minette, which they did, opening in early 1968.

"That summer, a tornado roared eastward down Seventh Street and took the roof off of their plant. The president of the company called me from Cleveland, Ohio, and said, 'Jimmy, why didn't you tell me about your tornadoes? How often do you have them?' I told him truthfully that this was the first one we had ever had that did any damage. Whether he believed me or not I don't know, but they put the roof back on and started operation again.

"The company made fordiner wire, which was a cloth that strained the pulp in paper mills which made fine quality paper. The cloth was made of copper and was rather expensive. The German-made machinery they used to produce the wire was also very expensive.

"It was their first plant in the Southeast and was very successful until their own ingenuity put them out of business. The copper wire lasted only a few months and had to be replaced, thus keeping the company busy with repeat sales. However, they developed a system to make wire out of synthetics that lasted much longer, making the plant unprofitable.

"An industrial bond issue was also provided the company for several million dollars. They later sold their building to a Chattanooga, Tennessee, firm which, after several months, closed the plant leaving a fine building of ninety-six thousand square feet vacant."

Thus ended another interesting industry story involving Faulkner.

Colt Industries

Faulkner's political involvement provided the contact to land yet another industrial company for his hometown.

"I was a delegate to the Democratic National Convention in Miami in the summer of 1972 where I met the long-time sergeant-at-arms for the United States Senate, Bob Dumphy. We became friends and soon thereafter, he retired to Florida.

"About 1974, he called me and asked me if I would do him a favor. He said he had a friend in Connecticut who wanted to meet some bankers and other important people in New Orleans and asked if I would meet him there. I agreed to do this.

"During the meeting in New Orleans the gentleman learned of my interest in industrial development. I had forgotten about the incident when he called me about three years later. He said, 'Jimmy, I remember your interest in industrial development and I have a lead for you. I was in the legal office of Colt Industries last week and their subsidiary, Holley Carburetor, is looking for a site for building in the Southeast.' He told me that I could find the gentleman in charge of the search at a motel in Montgomery. This was on Friday. I called the man on the phone and asked him when he could come to Bay Minette to look at a building, and he said he could come the next morning, which was Saturday.

"The person with the keys to the site lived in Mobile and I wasn't sure that I could find him, but I did. The gentleman came down to see the building and liked it. A few days later Holley Carburetor officials came to look at the building and agreed that they wanted it, promising to employ four hundred to five hundred people.

"They had a contract with Ford Motor Company to make about four hundred and sixty thousand special type carburetors a year and were ready to get into production. I got Eastwood Nealley to agree on the price of $1.1 million, which was a real bargain, and they said they would get their machinery out right away. The plant was down to twenty-eight employees by then.

"However, a few days later I got a call from the manager of Holley telling me that Ford Motor Company had canceled the contract and therefore they could not use the building, but asked if we would be willing to let them have it for another subsidiary that would employ only seventy-five people. Naturally, being disappointed, I figured seventy-five jobs was better than nothing. They were going to take it up with the Colt board of directors who told them they were not in the real estate business. Besides, they said they had another subsidiary looking for a location in the Southeast. After two or three days looking, they decided they would put a Quincy Compressor plant here. Quincy Compressor's headquarters is in Quincy, Illinois.

"Colt Industries announced in January 1980 that Quincy Compressor Division had agreed to purchase the Eastwood Nealley building and they were going to put a plant in Bay Minette. This was done and the company has been a very fine citizen ever since, employing some two hundred forty or more people, and continues to grow.

"They manufacture air compressor machines and components and started operation here in 1981, under the able management of president Ken Rollins. They have expanded several times and, in 1998, they announced a new expansion of four thousand square feet and an expenditure for additional equipment. The investment in machinery and expansion amounted to over one million dollars."

Jinan

Local industry received an international flavor in 1990 with a firm that had its roots in China.

"We were dealing with a Chinese gentleman and a group from Columbus, Ohio, about the possibility of putting a marble processing plant here. The marble was to come from China and they would make various products that would be shipped throughout the United States.

"After several months and a couple of visits to Ohio, the plant failed to materialize.

"However, this gentleman told us about another Chinese company from Jinan Province of Shandon, China, that was looking for a possible plant site or distribution center.

"On December 4, 1990, officials of the company, including the president, visited Bay Minette and agreed to lease the eighteen-thousand-square-foot building behind Den-Tal-Ez that belongs to the Industrial Development Board of the city of Bay Minette. The board had acquired it from the expiration of the fifteen-year bond issue to build their plant, and the agreement had been that at the end of that time this building, or equivalent, would belong to the Board.

"After several months of red tape, the lease was signed for a little over three thousand dollars per month and several Chinese citizens moved here to start distributing fine electric lathes of various sizes and costs.

"Their home plant in Jinan, China, employed eight thousand people and they wanted an assembly and distribution service plant in Bay Minette. The operation was successful in a small way for several years but, because of problems in China of getting parts for the machinery they sold in the U.S., they gradually had to fold up their local operation.

"This was unfortunate because the machinery was a good seller at a reasonable price but, of course, they had to have parts for service.

"The Chinese people were impressed with the friendly people in Bay Minette and were glad they had selected our town. The local people enjoyed their presence and getting to know the ways of the Chinese people.

"Jim Reidler of the Alabama Development Office worked hard with us on this lathe company and he was very helpful in getting them to locate here. The president of the China plant paid two or three visits here and was always very courteous and insisted on giving some of the local people a dinner at a Chinese restaurant in Mobile.

"Even after they agreed to come here, it was a long ordeal getting approval from the Chinese government to locate here. If you think the American government has a lot of red tape, you don't know anything until you get to dealing with China. About thirty different agencies had to approve the move."

Holland Industrial Services

Small industries have provided a stable diversity for Bay Minette. One such facility came as a result of an expansion from the nearby community of Stapleton, Faulkner notes.

"Dan Holland had put in a small operation in Stapleton in 1992 where he specialized in repair and re-manufacturing of electrical switch gears and transformers. His business opportunities were good and he became interested in a larger building and moved to Bay Minette.

"He first contacted me in April 1994, as his father had suggested. His father, Carl, was a long-time friend and official of Kaiser Industries, who also lived in Stapleton.

"Holland had learned that the property on Rabun Road had been obtained by the Industrial Development Board, free of charge, when an attempt had been made to attract the marble manufacturing industry. That industry had purchased seven acres but later, when things did not work out, they gave the property to the Industrial Development Board.

"After much negotiation and ironing out of problems, everything was lined up and in April of 1997, ground was broken for the plant. The company is small, but has done well and continues to enlarge its operations. Primarily, Holland Industrial Services re-manufactures electrical power distribution equipment for pulp, paper, and chemical industries.

"Holland said he chose to keep his business in Bay Minette because this area became his roots, and also he liked Bay Minette and Baldwin County because the Industrial Board, the Chamber of Commerce, and city officials stay on top of things and helped him in every way they could. He also was complimentary of our school system that provided a good education for his children.

"This is another fine, but small industry of which the area is proud," Faulkner boasts.

Gulf Packaging Company

Sometimes the location of a large industry can lead to the development of a smaller plant for the area. This was the case of Gulf Packaging Company, Faulkner relates.

"In 1990, Larry Taylor became the owner of Gulf Packaging Company, Incorporated. He located his plant on a small tract of land with a four thousand-square-foot building on Nicholsville Road. The property belonged to the Industrial Development Board of the city of Bay Minette.

"In a sense, this operation was a result of International Paper Container Division moving to Bay Minette because Taylor worked for them and saw the need of erecting a plant that could produce smaller quantities than IP could do profitably.

"So, with the cooperation of local citizens, he obtained this land and started off working about five people. Since opening, he has made several expansions and is presently employing about thirty-five or forty.

"Not long after he started his business it expanded to the point that he needed additional capital and he merged with another company in order to supply his continually growing list of customers.

"It was in 1993 that Taylor's company decided it needed to expand, and at the time they needed about three hundred thousand dollars for the project they wanted. The Industrial Board helped them in every way possible and suggested various ways the plant might be financed, but he received local funds and added a fifteen thosuand-square-foot building, which tripled his manufacturing area.

"The company serves markets such as furniture, filters, computers, paper, chemical companies, agriculture, and many small specialty manufacturers. They have a full service facility with custom design capabilities and serve a market of approximately 150 miles from Bay Minette and he uses his own truck fleet.

"Gulf Packaging has done well, and they continue to expand and operate in Bay Minette. It is a good, local, civic-minded industry of which local people are proud."

Cedartown Paper Board Cores

Persistence continued to pay off for Faulkner in the location of a paperboard core plant for his hometown.

"It took five years of constant selling before the firm was persuaded to move their small operation in Prichard, Alabama, to Bay Minette in 1983.

"Fortunately, the Industrial Development Board owned eight acres of land on the Fort Morgan branch of the L&N Railroad and Nicholsville Road which was made available to them at a reasonable cost.

"Darroll Freeman of Cedartown, Georgia, was the president and owner of the company and became a good friend of mine, and listened to our persuasion to put his plant in Bay Minette.

"His first manager here was Robert Sullivan from nearby Crossroads, making it possible to have the operation close by his home. They built a building of fifty thousand square feet with a railroad spur serving them. The required capital for this initial operation was approximately $1 million.

"The company manufactures and converts heavy paper rolls for the paper industry, such as spiral tubes and cores of various sizes. The company ships in paper and converts it to these tubes or rolls.

"The starting employment was about thirty in 1983. The company officials stated they would like to expand their plant with another fifty thousand-square-foot building, employing more people.

"In 1997, the conversion was started and they employed forty people.

"About this time they merged with a large national company known as Newark Paper Board Cores.

"At one time I owned the radio station in Cedartown, which gave me a helpful connection, but it still took five years of persuasion. Apparently, the company is very happy with their operation here and certainly the citizens of Bay Minette appreciate them as they are good, civic-minded, cooperative people."

Baldwin Asphalt

Faulkner maintains that nine out of ten prospects are more likely to locate their plant in an area that has an industrial park. He says the Industrial Development Board of Bay Minette has attempted to keep land available for prospective industries at a reasonable cost and, because of that, has been successful in getting several operations that would not have otherwise been able to locate in the city.

"Such a case was the Baldwin Asphalt Company, which purchased land on the Fort Morgan branch of the L & N Railroad and Nicholsville Road. Later they purchased an adjoining eighteen acres from the Industrial Development Board, giving them a total of over thirty acres. They have put most of it into use, producing asphalt for highways in nearby counties.

"This facility, at the time, was owned by three construction contracting companies: Billingsly Construction and G. S. Warner

& Company, both of Mobile, and Gunn Construction in Birmingham.

"They erected a modern facility and have continued to expand and do well in the area and give employment to thirty-five or forty people, including truck operators, asphalt spreaders, and other affiliated operations.

"They are another small company that adds to the diversification and solidity of the manufacturing industries in Bay Minette," Faulkner affirms.

Yellow Hammer Building Systems

The far-sighted planning of the Bay Minette Industrial Board in obtaining land often proved decisive in locating new industry. The board placed the city in a distinct advantage by having property in hand, and being willing to offer it at a reasonable price. This proved true again in October 1995 when several people arrived in the city wanting to see about obtaining land to start an industry here.

"After months of persuading them that Bay Minette was the proper location for them they purchased fifty-one acres of land on Highway 31 South, near Den-Tal-Ez, for their operation. It was possible to locate them here because the board, in prior years, had purchased the so-called 'Lawson Field' and had this much acreage remaining, some of which was not level, but was ideal for this operation.

"Groundbreaking for Yellow Hammer Building Systems was held in November 1995," noted Faulkner.

"The name Yellow Hammer was selected because it is the name of Alabama's state bird. The company owned operations in Canada and Virginia and these plants were named after state birds also.

"The purpose of the plant was to build modular homes and

other related building components. Norman Berneche was owner and CEO of the plant and moved with his family to a beautiful home here in Bay Minette where he has been pleased with the community, as well as his operations.

"He still remains excited about the prospects and success of Yellow Hammer. One of his partners was Ralph Grisham of Daphne, and they went into production in 1996.

"In addition to modular homes, they manufacture wall panels, trusses, kit homes, and other related building components.

"The beautiful homes which they produce at a reasonable price are exported to parts of Georgia, Florida, Mississippi, Tennessee, and South Carolina. They have a capacity to turn out several hundred homes per year and they employ about twenty people. However, much of their production is sub-contracted to such local companies as plumbers, electricians, and bricklayers.

"It is another small company that seems to be doing well in Bay Minette in which the owners, as well as local people, are pleased," Faulkner added.

Barclay

Jimmy Faulkner has always been quick to follow through on industrial development prospect tips, whatever the source. Occasionally his own family provided such a prospect.

"Early in the 1980s my son, Wade, had a friend, Joe Dzwonkowski, who told him that he was looking for a place to put an industry in Florida. Wade suggested he come to see me in Bay Minette, which he did.

"On his visit to Bay Minette, Joe explained he wanted to put in a dimensional woods products plant and needed about ten acres of land. He was shown the land on White Avenue Extension, where the Industrial Development Board of the city of Bay Minette owned about sixty acres at the time. He selected twelve acres and eventually erected his factory.

"An industrial development bond for two million dollars was arranged for him and the First National Bank in Montgomery financed it. The plant was erected and had some difficulty because of economics, but was gradually working out its problems. They employed eighty people and seemed to be on the way to success.

"Unfortunately, the bank in Montgomery wanted to foreclose on the plant because Barclay, which was the eventual name, had faltered on some payments. It, however, was clearly understood that if payments were missed that they would be added on to the end of the mortgage and the plant would be allowed to continue to run.

"However, the bank decided otherwise and took it to court and, amazingly, a local attorney helped the bank. By using misleading information, they caused the plant to close. This cost the Bay Minette area over eighty jobs. This was a big disappointment and proved that, in spite of how hard you work, unfair people can cause bad things to happen," Faulkner concluded.

Bay Minette Mills, Incorporated

Before the advent of industrial development bonds in Alabama, interested citizens of Bay Minette came together in March 1953, to form a corporation to assist the city's economy.

"Bay Minette Mills, Incorporated, was a private tax-paying corporation under the state laws of Alabama. Its purpose was to encourage, maintain and support business and civic interest in Bay Minette and surrounding areas.

"Even though tax paying, the corporation was a non-profit development company and assisted a number of businesses to get started and stay in operation in Bay Minette.

"In 1953, with the contributions of local citizens of over $60,000, the corporation constructed a brick building which was leased to The Well Made Pants Company of Baltimore, Maryland, and its owner, Manny Pleet, for the purpose of manufacturing quality men's trousers.

"The building was actually financed by the sale of a total of sixty-eight thousand dollars worth of stock to two hunded fifty local stockholders. The purchase of the stock by local citizens was one of the most cooperative and sacrificial efforts ever accomplished locally.

"The development company was used to assist the pants factory and later, when the Standard Furniture plant burned to the ground in December 1959, it made it possible for Standard to borrow $125,000 from the Small Business Administration and build a new thirty thousand-square-foot building to keep the company in operation.

"In the 1980s, the corporation was no longer needed as laws had been changed in Alabama permitting industrial bonds to serve the same purpose," Faulkner noted.

"The pants factory was the first industry brought to Alabama after the formation of Alabama Department of Economic and Community Affairs. The Alabama Development Office was an offspring of ADECA in 1963.

"I was a state senator at the time and was able to get their appropriation increased. Subsequently, they had a prospect from North Carolina and they sent them to see me in Bay Minette. At the time, the only other industrial plant in Bay Minette was Newport Industries."

Baldwin Pole and Piling

Following the construction of a huge sawmill by Ray E. Loper

Lumber Company, Mr. A. K. Easley of Monroe County came to Bay Minette in the 1950s, looking for a site to construct a pole-peeling plant.

"I accompanied Mr. Easley and we virtually covered the county looking at the possibilities of timber that would furnish his proposed plant with sufficient poles to maintain a good operation.

"Mr. Easley determined that there was ample supply of timber, and built his plant on Highway 31 North, just east of the L&N Railroad. The plant was very successful and they also went into the creosote and pole treating business to serve the electrical industry throughout the Southeast.

"After Mr. Easley died, the plant was operated by his sons, Ted and Mabrey, and Willison Duck, his son-in-law. The plant continued successful operation for many years and eventually was sold to Tom McMillan of Stockton, who has operated the plant since and has continuously employed about fifty people.

"The Easleys were good citizens, as is McMillan, and the plant is another small industry that has served Bay Minette well, not only in employment, but in furnishing a high price market for our timber growers," Faulkner said.

Marble Manufactures of America

Not every industrial adventure proved successful. Jimmy Faulkner remembers one that never really got off the ground.

"Marble Manufacturers of America was the only manufacturer of marble trophy bases in the United States. In 1983 they announced that they wanted to build a plant in Bay Minette. Saralyn and Dale Buck and their family of Lowndes County, Alabama, had borrowed and invested $400,000 or $500,000 to build a plant. They spent most of the money purchasing a machine from Italy that would cut the marble as needed for the industry.

"Sales of the product were no problem. However, the trouble came when the Italian machine company sent a man to Bay Minette who could not speak English and he was not able to get the machine to produce as guaranteed. The delay caused the Bucks to lose all they had. Thus, a productive, very successful business, which would have employed about twenty-five people and aided the local economy, was not able to make a go of it.

"The Italian company, in the meantime, went into bankruptcy and this spelled the doom of the bright idea," Faulkner added.

Ray E. Loper Lumber Company

Jimmy Faulkner's brother provided a valuable tip that led to yet another major industry for the Bay Minette area.

"In the early 1950s, my brother Thurston was the vocational agriculture teacher in Fayette, Alabama. He and Paul Corwin, who married a Bay Minette girl, Lauda Leak, went together to purchase the *Northwest Alabamian* newspaper. Paul, who became editor, had been the editor of the *Baldwin Times,* which I owned.

"They called to tell me that Ray E. Loper of Brown Lumber Company of Louisville, Kentucky, who had a big operation in Fayette, was planning to move to south Mississippi to establish a new operation.

"I got them to persuade Loper to pay a visit to Bay Minette, which he did.

"He and Mrs. Loper came here with two friends from Birmingham and J. B. Blackburn and I took them fishing on his boat in the lakes north of Stockton. While here, he was persuaded that we had a lot of timberland and Graham Brown, the owner, agreed. Loper later moved to Bay Minette where he started buying timberland.

"One of his first purchases was eight thousand acres from Henry Bryars for which he paid thirty-two dollars per acre. Local people thought he was crazy for paying such a high price. In the coming months, Brown, with Ray Loper as local manager and part owner, purchased some forty thousand acres in Mobile, Baldwin, Monroe, and Escambia counties.

"In addition, he built a huge sawmill in Bay Minette which, at one time, employed about three hundred people, including those in the mill and in the woods furnishing the logs.

"Eventually the sawmill closed but in 1983, Brownwood Preserving opened a pole plant here where they cut the poles on their own timber, as well as buying poles from other sources, peeling them, or shipping them to either Tuscaloosa or Louisville, Kentucky, for processing.

"The venture was very successful as there were several oil wells discovered in Escambia County and the company received high lease rates for much of their other land in Baldwin and Mobile counties.

"Loper lived in Bay Minette in a fine home for several years, handling the timber lands and selling some. In the meantime, the land got to be so valuable he refused to sell any of it for less than two thousand dollars an acre. One tract in Monroe County, for which he paid three dollars per acre for three thousand acres, he later sold for sixteen million dollars.

"The success of Loper's ingenious ability to recognize opportunities resulted in the James Graham Brown Foundation eventually being worth some two hundred million dollars, of which Loper was chairman of the board, and was in complete control of the timberland.

"As he grew older, he moved to Tuscaloosa, enjoying life well into his nineties. His foundation has made several gifts to the Bay Minette area and at one time gave one million dollars to the University of Alabama, and other gifts, including about thirty acres of land in the city of Bay Minette, for industrial purposes. Most of his gifts, however, went to Kentucky where Brown's will stated that the majority of his estate's earnings would be given.

"I always argued with Loper that forty-nine percent of that much money was a whole lot. But compared to the amount given in Kentucky, Alabama has received a very small amount. Presently the Brown and Loper timber holdings in the area are down to seven thousand acres.

"Loper was a good citizen and is a good friend of mine. His son, Graham Brown, lives in Mobile and still maintains his contacts and interest in the projects of this area. He succeeded his father on the foundation board in Louisville but a vast majority of the members are from Kentucky.

"This company's venture into this area did more to establish good prices for land than can be imagined. The telephone call from my brother and Corwin proved to be a great thing for this area," Faulkner remembers.

Den-Tal-Ez

When Jimmy Faulkner came to Bay Minette in 1936, the only plant in the city was Newport Industries, which had been there since 1913 and employed about two hundred people. Bacon-McMillan veneer plant in Stockton employed around one hundred and thirty. In addition, there were a few sawmills around the area. Since that time, Faulkner has been instrumental in locating many diverse industries in the area.

"Industrial prospects occasionally come from unusual circumstances. In 1968, Governor George Wallace was running for president. He relied upon me to line up airplanes to fly him on campaign trips. He was frightened of flying and preferred jets that could fly at high altitudes.

"He had a campaign appearance scheduled and wanted me to get a plane for the trip. I got the jets from a company in Oklahoma City, Oklahoma. The plane was not available, as the pilot said he had to take an industrial group to Florida to look for a site to build a new plant.

"After thinking about it, I asked Lowell Harrelson, a local contractor, to call the pilot and suggest he bring the prospects to Bay Minette. The pilot was instrumental in getting them here.

"They flew to Florida and on Wednesday morning, the pilot called stating they were going to land in Mobile that afternoon at 3 o'clock.

"Mrs. Martin located me in the lobby of First National Bank in Mobile, giving me only a few minutes warning, and obviously, I picked them up.

"Not knowing anything about the company, I had no idea whether they wanted to be in a small town or a city. Inviting members of the Mobile Area Chamber of Commerce, Harrelson and I fed them in the Bienville Club that night.

"We learned from the owner, Hal Pearson, an Auburn graduate from Uniontown, Alabama, that he wanted to be in a small town and we started selling him on Bay Minette. They visited and selected the site they preferred.

"Following their visit, Harrelson, Alabama Development Office Director Red Bamberg, Fred Denton with ADO, and I flew to Des Moines, Iowa, to recruit Den-Tal-Ez.

"Returning, through several negotiations, we were able to obtain twenty-seven acres from the Jack Robertson family for the plant.

"Den-Tal-Ez built an 18,000-square-foot building and soon had 52 employees in Bay Minette, while maintaining a staff of 225 in Des Moines. The Bay Minette facility produced the same amount as Des Moines, so the owners decided to move the entire operation here. An eighty thousand-square-foot building was then built with a two million dollar industrial bond, with the provision that at the end of fifteen years when the bonds were paid, they would pay the city a reasonable amount of money. In lieu thereof, they gave the building that later housed Jima, and three acres of land, to the Industrial Development Board.

"Den-Tal-Ez was later sold to Mr. Jeffrey Pearlman, who is continually trying to increase sales for the plant. They now employ about one hundred people.

"At one time Den-Tal-Ez produced fifty percent of all dental chairs in the United States. Dr. Joe Volker, who later became Chancellor of the University of Alabama in Birmingham, came down to the plant-opening here because the chairs were developed at the university. Den-Tal-Ez promised to build three more buildings to house research and development, office support and engineering. Mr. Pearlman promises to bring more departments here in the future."

Standard Furniture Manufacturing Company, Inc.

Bay Minette's largest and most successful industry is Standard Furniture Manufacturing Company, which is locally owned by the Hodgson family. The company makes fine, but economical, bedroom suites by the tens of thousands. In addition, they buy other furniture from all over the world, store it in Bay Minette, and ship it out with their locally produced furniture.

Jimmy Faulkner has fond memories of how it all began.

"It was in 1946 when W. M. Hodgson, Sr., a successful local businessman and Standard Oil Distributor, and I rode to Magnolia Springs for a political county organization meeting for Handy Ellis, lieutenant governor, who was running for governor. It was on this trip that he told me confidentially that he, Norman McInnis, Newton Beasley, and others were going to start a furniture plant here. To me, this was exciting news.

"They did so, and opened for operation in 1947, but it was not successful since their manner of production was not streamlined. As a result, Hodgson purchased the interests of the others and started modern production lines. Ever since, the company has continued to grow.

"His two sons, W. M. (Mac) Hodgson, Jr., and Robert (Bob) Hodgson, graduated from the University of Alabama and returned home to help their dad successfully manufacture bedroom suites. Even though they struggled in building up their business, they worked out many problems and continued to grow.

"However, a blow struck them in December 1959, when their building burned to the ground, with all its contents. They asked me to help get refinancing so they could rebuild and keep going.

"At this time, including trucks and all their other assets, they had a net of slightly over one hundred thousand dollars. Their attorney Norborne Stone, Mac, Bob, and I went to Atlanta to put in an application with the Small Business Administration for a $125,000 loan.

"Luckily, I had a friend who was Southeastern Manager of SBA and he was most helpful to us. He was Judge Charles Adams of Alexander City who had been speaker of the House of Representatives in Alabama and probate judge in Tallapoosa County. Also, U.S. Senator John Sparkman, who was the leader in America in the Small Business Administration, had gotten Adams appointed. He pitched in and helped us any way he could. Within seventeen days the loan was approved. At that time, this was the fastest approval of an SBA loan in history, and probably still stands today. You have to go through a lot of red tape to get such a loan.

"Standard's assets were hardly enough to warrant the loan, but fortunately Bay Minette Mills, Incorporated, which we had organized to help in such situations, had assets and, because of this, they were able to get the amount for which they asked. They used this money to build a thirty thousand-square-foot building on Highway 31 South, the original location, and they started making furniture again within several months.

"Like many industries, because of lack of financing, they did not own enough land. Since then, they have gradually purchased considerable additional land, continued to build additional buildings, and as of this date have some two million square feet of manufacturing and warehouse space under roof here in Bay Minette.

"They employ almost one thousand people and their gross income in 2000 was near two hundred million dollars, which makes them one of the hundred largest industries in Alabama.

"Both W. M. Sr., and Jr., have died and Mac's son, Billy, became president and Bob, his uncle, is chairman of the board. Bob's son, Phillip, is also a vice president and the three of them make a successful team. They have been intelligent enough to employ competent help.

"The success of this company is amazing and hopefully it will continue. The hard work and intelligence on the part of the Hodgson family will cause it to continue to grow."

W. M. Hodgson, Jr., who, with the rest of his family, was a good friend of Faulkner, often was quoted as saying that if it had not been for Jimmy Faulkner, Standard Furniture would not be here today.

"That's not exactly true," Faulkner insists, "although I was able to help on occasion when called upon. The real reason Standard Furniture is here and is successful is entirely through the genius and hard work of the W. M. Hodgson, Sr., family."

Small Projects — Daphne Elementary School

Jimmy Faulkner learned early in his business career that one has to ask for, push and shove, to get things done. This is true with small projects just as it is true with larger industrial prospects.

"It has always been my desire to do everything possible to make Bay Minette and Baldwin County a better place to live. If I have been successful in a small way, it is because of my persistence and willingness to ask others to help us. In this respect, I have been able to get some things accomplished that would not have been accomplished had I sat back and done nothing.

"One example is the elementary school at Daphne. It was in 1938 that Frank Dixon was elected governor and I was his county campaign manager, along with Judge G. W. Robertson and Dr. W. C. (Buddy) Holmes.

"Alabama had five, what was called, 'normal' colleges. Actually, they were two-year institutions and were located in Daphne, Troy, Livingston, Florence, and Jacksonville, Alabama. Later they became teacher colleges, but Daphne was never successful because of the lack of students.

"Because of this failure, it was decided by the authorities that it should be closed. Governor Bibb Graves, prior to 1938, floated a bond issue in the legislature that would help build these colleges and Daphne's portion was $151,000. Since no one wanted to spend it on Daphne Normal, local citizens agreed that if the money could be spent by the Baldwin County Board of Education to build an elementary school in Daphne, they would agree to the closing proposal.

"I was asked by County Superintendent S. M. Tharpe and County Board of Education Chairman Frank Earle to go to Montgomery with them and ask Governor Dixon to approve this exchange.

"I had no difficulty getting an appointment with the governor and Governor Dixon approved the exchange, and the elementary school was built with this $151,000. At the time, it was the most beautiful and probably the best school building in Baldwin County, and continues to be so. However, some additions have been made and, of course, it has been kept in good condition. The building today would cost in the neighborhood of five million dollars.

"Aubrey McVay was principal of the school and asked me to give the commencement address to the first eighth grade graduating class. He later became county superintendent of education and has a building named in his honor at the local community college," Faulkner noted.

Paving, Drainage, Cemetery, and Ditches

Jimmy Faulkner's political connections at the State Capitol have often been helpful in obtaining state assistance for the Bay Minette area.

"During Governor James E. "Big Jim" Folsom's first term, which was 1946 to 1950, he was always very considerate of me and appointed me to state commissions. On occasion, I asked him to do things for Bay Minette, which he always did.

"For example, we got East Fifth Street paved, streets around the elementary and high schools, as well as the Old Daphne Road and the road to Newport Industries. Also, we four-laned D'Olive Street from the courthouse west to Highway 59, and the north side of the courthouse, which had never been paved.

"Also, the Bay Minette Cemetery had always been a mess and, upon request, he sent two big truck loads of convicts from Atmore prison and they worked many days putting the cemetery into good condition, and it has remained so ever since.

"In addition, we had standing water on the northwest side of

Bay Minette between McMillan Avenue and what is now Highway 59. Folsom had two big flatbed truck loads of prisoners sent down here and for many weeks they dug out ditches to drain what is now a good residential area. If this had not been done, the area still would be wetlands. Fortunately, this opened up many acres for development," Faulkner noted.

Other Projects

Faulkner also used his close association with Governor George C. Wallace to get assistance for his hometown and county.

"While he was governor, he granted several requests to improve conditions here, including drainage of the southwest portion of the courthouse square, which always flooded after a big rain. Water would often go into buildings, including the Alabama Power Company's local office. This project drained the square and also improved drainage down D'Olive Street, which helped the entire area.

"Governor Wallace also had the state highway department four-lane Crossroads Road from Highway 59 about two miles west, which eased traffic in the Douglasville area of Bay Minette, and he also gave us funds to enable the Bay Minette Housing Authority to obtain federal funds.

"Governor Wallace gave us $170,000 to buy eight acres of land to the west of the college land on the highway where now two beautiful white buildings stand. He also gave us two million dollars to build the Gary Branch building. He also gave us enough money to put an auditorium and a gym at Perdido school, as well as money for schools in Elberta, Elsanor, Rosinton, and others. None of this would have been done if he had not been urged to do it.

"In addition to this, he gave us three hundred thousand dollars to light Highway 31 from D'Olive Street west to the city line.

"Sometimes, it is amazing what you can get if you ask for it. Too, you get a lot of turn downs."

Pleasure Island

The story of how Pleasure Island, the tourist mecca of sandy beaches and rolling Gulf surf, got its name is one of the most interesting of Jimmy Faulkner's influence.

"Governor Folsom had appointed me to serve on the eleemosynary committee for the state of Alabama. I was one of three members of this committee that had the responsibility of inspecting the state's eleemosynary institutions, such as the prisons, insane hospitals, and such. It was during one of these inspections near Birmingham at the delinquent girls prison that I rode with Folsom to Birmingham.

"Folsom had asked me to dinner and, during the conversation, made the comment that the land below the intercoastal canal, Fort Morgan and Perdido Pass, was an island, and if I would think of a name, he would proclaim it such.

"Having already thought of it, I wrote the name down on a piece of paper and slipped it into his pocket, realizing that under his condition at the time, he might not remember it.

"In about two weeks, he signed a governor's proclamation naming the area 'Pleasure Island,'" Faulkner smiles.

Hand Avenue Extension

Often a person can work hard knowing that all he is doing is speeding up a project that might be done some day. On the other hand, one can work on some improvements that would never have been done without pushing.

Faulkner gives two examples that were small projects illustrating each of the above points.

"During Governor Albert Brewer's administration, a local citizen, Marion Wilkins, was his highway director. I approached them about extending the four-lanes of Hand Avenue from the North Baldwin Hospital north to the four-way stop, a distance of less than one mile.

"Wilkins got his engineers to make an estimate of what the project would cost. At the time it was some four hundred thousand dollars.

"Brewer was not re-elected and he was not able to finish the four-lane. Ray Bass, highway director for Governor George Wallace, was favorable to the project, but was never able to set aside the money to do it.

"Several times the street was to be completed but something always delayed it. Many years passed, and nothing happened.

"It was in 1994 that Governor Fob James was elected for his second term. Bass, a career highway engineer, remembered his desire to finish the project. He worked with the new director Jimmy Butts. By this time the cost had more than doubled to around $1 million. However, the work is now completed and gives a much nicer entrance on the north to downtown Bay Minette," Faulkner stated.

Faulkner believes the extension of Hand Avenue was obviously so important that it would have eventually been done, but who knows when?

Highway 31 South Lighting

Another highway project was boulevard-type lighting on Highway 31 from the D'Olive Street intersection south to the Bay Minette city limits. Faulkner recalls the history of this project.

"Ray Bass, highway director under Governor Wallace, with the governor's approval, promised that this lighting would be done.

They kept putting it off, as certainly it was not absolutely essential, even though an important improvement to the safety of the people. Finally, the city asked Bass if they would pay for the engineering, would he go ahead with the project. He agreed and eventually it was completed," Faulkner stated.

Although not many small cities have such highway lighting through town, this three hundred thousand dollar project added considerably to the attractiveness and safety of travelers.

Faulkner believes that although the lighting might have been done eventually, it would not have been completed by now, or perhaps ever.

Southern Aluminum Castings

Faulkner believes that one of his most successful efforts to get a good industry to locate in Bay Minette was the case of Southern Aluminum Castings, which makes sand aluminum castings for the automobile industry.

"When Den-Tal-Ez was persuaded to move to Bay Minette, Jim Hunt, his father and brothers, owned a small casting plant for the purpose of serving Den-Tal-Ez.

"Jim Hunt, who at the time was a CPA in Sarasota, Florida, decided to erect the plant in this area rather than Panama City, Florida, which he had been considering.

"Hal Pearson was president of Den-Tal-Ez and I approached him with the humble request that he tell Jim Hunt that if he wanted to sell him aluminum castings, he had to put his plant in Bay Minette. He did this and started off employing fifteen people. This was in 1973.

"As time passed, Jim continued to expand his plant and gradually got to the point he was using almost one hundred percent of his plant's capacity to serve Ford Motor Company, as he had made his company one of the acceptable suppliers for Ford.

"His sales continued to climb and expansions were required almost beyond his financial ability. Finally, in 1999, he sold his company to Citation and they have expanded it further and are presently employing around six hundred people.

"The people at Southern Aluminum (now Citation) have been good citizens and have furnished steady employment at a good payscale for all of these local people," Faulkner notes.

Southern Molding

Where most of the plants that located in Bay Minette have succeeded, many beyond expectations, not all have. Such a case was Southern Molding of York, Alabama.

"In 1988, three men, Frank Newhauser, Peter Cecchini, Jr., and Ira B. Pruitt came to Bay Minette interested in putting a small manufacturing plant here. The idea originated through my good friend Tom Newhauser, who was really the backbone of the operation and owned plants in York.

"The Industrial Development Board of the city of Bay Minette purchased ten acres of land on the corner of Nicholsville Road and Dickman Road, joining the Fort Morgan branch of the L&N Railroad.

"Finally an agreement was made and they purchased five acres and erected two small buildings. Frank Newhauser was put in charge of constructing machinery to make plugs to go into the ends of paper rolls. The idea was to use wood pulp, heated and molded into plugs.

"Unfortunately, the machinery never worked as well as needed, nor did the sales develop. Several things were tried, but never with a great deal of success.

"Finally, the owners gave up and put the two buildings and plant up for sale or lease."

Bay Minette Housing Authority

It was a Sunday morning that would change the lives forever of many of Bay Minette's African American residents. It was in the early 1960s and the rain was steadily pelting the top of Jimmy Faulkner's car. The wipers swept back and forth, clearing a path on the windshield as Faulkner turned down the muddy street of the section of town known as Douglasville.

"I saw ladies and gentlemen, dressed in their Sunday best, wading through the mud going to Union Baptist Church. I made up my mind then and there that if there was anything I could possibly do about it, I was going to correct such a deplorable situation," Faulkner remembered.

"At the time, we only had twenty-three standard homes in our black community, including Douglasville and the Brownwood area. There were no streetlights, no pavement, no sidewalks and there were open ditches.

"The matter was discussed with the city council, with little success in the beginning, but finally with arguing and persuading, they agreed that if I would become chairman they would appoint a housing authority and we would see what could be done. Thus, we got our start.

"At the time, there was a national program called Neighborhood Re-development. There were only seven cities in the southeast selected and we happened to be one of them, others being cities like Miami and New Albany, Mississippi. We were the smallest.

"The program provided that the federal government would put up seventy-five percent of funds available to build new houses, refurbish old ones, pave the streets, clean the ditches, and make other general improvements. The other twenty-five percent was to be furnished by local government either 'in kind' or cash.

"We got small appropriations in the beginning and managed to show some improvements and gradually the program accelerated. Over a period of twenty-five years, with the assistance of the city with Harry Still, Jr., and with administrators such as Charles Barton, Steve McMillan, Harry Still, Sr., Harold Jones, and Jack Jones, we were able to get over twelve million dollars spent in Douglasville, Brownwood division, and white areas south of the railroad.

"If the state would spend money improving the highways along any of this area, we could count twenty-five percent of it that touched our project as our local part. Thus, I persuaded Governor Wallace and his highway director to widen the street from Highway 31 towards Crossroads to four lanes and this gave us several thousand dollars of matching funds.

"As we went along, many obstacles had to be overcome, including public sentiment. Amazingly, the biggest opposition came from the black community because they simply could not believe that white people wanted to do them a favor. With the able assistance of the Douglasville High School Principal, Leroy Bryant, we were able to overcome this opposition and after they saw what was being done and all, they were all for it.

"At first, they said they disapproved of our project because they said we were trying to include too much land. Bay Minette people like space and we had our lots bigger than most towns, but they granted it and soon we ran out of land and had to buy additional property and it has now also been filled.

"About one third of the way through the program, we asked for an appropriation of six hundred thousand dollars for the following year. An engineer out of Montgomery, Steve McMillan, and I went to Atlanta. There, we were told they couldn't give us that much since they were giving about eleven million dollars to Miami, and cut our appropriation to three hundred thousand dollars.

"I explained to them that they had made us a promise that they would support us in Bay Minette and they wanted one smaller city for an example to other cities in the United States. However, if they were not going to give us the six hundred thousand dollars, they could take it all and keep it and give the rest of it to Miami, which would not notice it one way or the other.

"I had to leave. After I walked out of the room, the government official asked Steve and the engineer if I was just kidding and they said, 'You better believe he's not.' We got the six hundred thousand dollars and were able to continue the program, which has given Bay Minette one of the finest quality housing programs in the United States, with less than two percent below standard (standard being minimum FHA requirements).

"After twenty-five years as chairman, I resigned, and presently serving as chairman and Housing Authority members are: Winters Thomas, chairman; Melvin Fleming, Eugenia Trawick, George Watkins, and Jason Padgett."

Bay Minette Airport

One of the most difficult tasks Faulkner undertook was getting Bay Minette an airport.

"After the war, Bay Minette did not have any place for airplanes to land and it became very important that this be corrected. This area is not conducive to long, level landing strips and thus it was very difficult to find a piece of land that would work. Thanks go to Connor Owens, a local attorney, who pointed out a location on Seventh Street, about one-and-a-half miles from the city limits: not perfect, but better than anything else. Fortunately, the land was available.

"The city appointed an Airport Authority composed of Willison Duck, Bob Hodgson, Lowell Harrelson, and me. We managed to scrape up enough money to get a thirty-six hundred-foot runway without any parking area or anything else. However, it did furnish a place for small planes to land.

"Over the years, demands for a better airport were ever present, but thanks to the changing rules and regulations of the FAA, it was very difficult to accomplish. FAA did promise us that if we would get started on an improvement program, which included lengthening the runway to forty-three hundred feet, pushing the parking ramp back three hundred feet from the runway, and lighting the runway, that they would stick with us until this was done.

"We got money from FAA to move the parking ramp back first. They furnished a small amount and we obtained the rest of the money, twenty thousand dollars from the state Aviation Commission, Baldwin County gave twenty thousand dollars, Ray E. Loper gave twenty thousand and the city did most of the work.

"The next move was to get the runway extended to 4,300 feet and lights added. We had to have more land and International Paper Company gave us one hundred fifty-nine acres.

"In the meantime, FAA changed their rules and regulations and we had to comply with them. For example, we had to have land for a crosswind runway, ascertain there would be at least seventy-five landings and take-offs on the field with planes above twelve thousand pounds, which included planes such as King Air, Beachcraft, and heavier. I personally called and wrote state industries throughout the area, getting them to write a letter saying that they were sure they would make so many landings here each year, some as few as a couple, some as many as four or five.

"Then Joel Clark resigned as a pilot from the U.S. Army Air Force and became the first full-time fixed base operator. He managed to build a building and for several years has repaired airplanes and given other maintenance and fuel services. Along the way, four or five hangars were built, but nothing has been done to improve the situation of major importance since the lighting. The state did approve, and we were able to get an improved instrument landing system, as well as improved lighting. Fortunately, efforts are on the way now for further improvements with the main goal being to extend the runway to five thousand feet. Bay Minette is the only city of like size in this area without a runway of five thousand feet.

"Thanks to Congressman Sonny Callahan, we have been given $150,000 a year for three years, with a possibility of other funds. In addition, he got us an appropriation of $4.5 million to improve the airport, about one million of which was spent in 2001. It will take one or two years to upgrade the facility to modern standards.

"About two years ago, the city appointed a legal Bay Minette Airport Authority composed of seven citizens. When I was chairman, we only served in an advisory position and did not have any legal authority, although the city always went along with our suggestions and helped when they could."

Bay Minette Hospital

After World War II, one of Bay Minette's most serious problems was the lack of a hospital. Dr. Percy Bryant, after much persuasion, put in a small clinic with a few patient rooms at the corner of Hand Avenue and Third Street. The wooden frame building still stands.

"Dr. Bryant finally tired of this operation, which overworked him and probably was not very profitable, and the citizens got together and managed to get enough money to buy equipment and establish the Mattie L. Rhodes Hospital, which was located where the new Civic Center is now.

"The beautiful home was built during the Depression by Mr. and Mrs. L. T. Rhodes, Sr., and she had a wide reputation as a fine, lovely lady and kept and rented rooms in sort of a modified bread-and-breakfast for a number of years. They finally died and the estate let a group buy it.

"We were able to buy enough hospital equipment out of Florida to equip twelve or fifteen rooms, plus a small operating room and other facilities, for about thirty-five thousand dollars. This money was raised locally. Two or three doctors owned the hospital and finally Dr. George Halliday took over and operated it for a number of years until we could get the present Hill-Burton facility erected.

"That came about after we formed a hospital committee to try to raise the funds, and they made me chairman. I went to Montgomery and was able to get sufficient Hill-Burton funds to build the two-story, fifty-bed facility located on Hand Avenue on twenty acres of land in 1965.

"The hospital board was able to complete the facility and for a number of years it served a good purpose, saving the lives of many people as well as taking care of them during their illnesses. However, one of the difficulties was getting enough doctors to take care of the needs. This gradually has improved over the years.

"One of the big disappointments during this time was that we were able to get sufficient Hill-Burton funds to build a 120-bed nursing home at a local cost of only ninety thousand dollars. This was toward the last of Hill-Burton funds available and we were very fortunate to get them.

"Unfortunately, before we could get the funds the local physicians had to approve it. Dr. Tyler Nichols, who was chairman, opposed it and we lost the funds and did not get a nursing home for many years, and then only sixty beds.

"In order to get sufficient funds to build the North Baldwin Hospital, I came up with the idea of getting a two-mill ad valorem tax passed in the first seven precincts of the county. The legislators made this a constitutional amendment and it was defeated the first time. After waiting a year, and with a better organization, we were able to pass it, and this has been in effect for about thirty years and has made a difference in the financing of the hospital.

"In the beginning, it only brought in about eighty thousand dollars a year, but has climbed to over four hundred thousand dollars presently. The tax expires unless renewed in a few years," Faulkner stated.

William F. Green Veterans Home

During the administration of Governor Guy Hunt the Veterans Administration decided it had enough funds to build sixty new veterans homes throughout the United States. Alabama was in desperate need of these facilities and was promised two of these nursing homes. The State Veterans Board wanted to build one in Huntsville and one in South Alabama. Mobile was the first proposed site for the South Alabama facility. Jimmy Faulkner was soon to become involved in its final location.

"The president of the University of South Alabama, Dr. Fred Whiddon, promised to give the board ten acres of land on their campus. However, when the funds were approved they contacted Dr. Whiddon and he changed his mind and would not give the veterans the land. They tried to see the mayor of Mobile, but were unable to do so. Then they became interested in Baldwin County.

"Well, about thirty years ago a very good friend of mine, A. G.

Allegri, Jr., had called me and wanted his sales manager, William F. Green, to be appointed to the State Veterans Board. Upon my recommendation, Governor George Wallace appointed him. Now, after Mobile had turned down the request, Michael Allegri, county commissioner and son of A. G. Allegri, Jr., brought Mr. Green to see me and reminded me that I got him appointed to the board and that now he was chairman of the state board.

"The delegation was looking for a ten-acre site for the home and we showed them a site on Highway 31 South. They liked it. The federal government had appropriated sufficient money to build a nine million to ten million dollar nursing home. However, the city of Bay Minette had to put up one-third of the cost. There was no way, at that time, the city could come up with the money.

"Coming up with local funding and the matter of time were the important issues. Governor Hunt was asked for state financial assistance but declared it could not be done at this time.

"I came up with an idea how Bay Minette could get their funds by arranging with the company that was going to operate the home to add a small amount to each patient until the funds could be paid off, and they would put up the money. This did not seem appropriate since we did not want the veterans to have to pay more than necessary.

"Then I went to see David Bronner, executive director of the state retirement system. I asked him if he would lend Bay Minette two and a half million dollars. He said, 'Jimmy, I can't waste my time lending two and a half million when I've got twenty-five *billion* dollars to worry about.' Then he smiled and said, 'This is important for Bay Minette to get this nursing home. Tell the city officials if they want to borrow the money from us, all they have to do is to write us a note just how much they want, how long they want to pay it, twenty years, thirty years, or whatever, and we will let

them have it. But remember, they must pay 8.75 percent interest.'
Of course, this was good news.

"Then, the remaining problem was time. The Veterans Administration had enough funds for only the sixty homes nationwide
and other states were standing in line, hoping that Alabama would
fail to qualify for our money. The Alabama Nursing Home Association knew this, and was trying to require the State Veterans Board
to get a Certificate of Need (CON) which would have required
from one to one-and-a-half years to do, and we would have lost the
home.

"Mr. Green went to Lieutenant Governor Jim Folsom and he
agreed the legislature would pass a bill stating the CON was not
necessary, and he had every reason to believe it was not needed.
However, on the last day of the legislative session, Folsom failed to
let the bill come up, and that killed it," Faulkner stated.

Meanwhile, anticipating a legal question, the legislature had
previously asked the Supreme Court for a ruling. Since the legislature failed to act, the request was returned without an opinion
saying it was then moot.

In desperation, Faulkner called the Chief Justice of the Supreme Court of Alabama, Sonny Hornsby.

Faulkner said, "Your honor, several years ago I called Judge
Richard Rives, Federal Judge of the Eleventh Circuit, and told him,
'Judge, I am not a lawyer so if I say something I shouldn't, please
stop me.' He said, 'Go ahead.' I told him what I wanted him to
know and he said 'stop.'

"So I told Judge Hornsby, 'Judge, I am not a lawyer and if I say
something I am not supposed to, please stop me.' He said, 'Go
ahead.' I then explained the situation about the two nursing homes
and stated that the Supreme Court did not rule that a CON was
necessary, which in my opinion it was not, and that we would lose

them to another state. He asked me several questions and finally said, 'This is very important to Alabama, let me think about it.'

"Of course, I did not expect him to give me an answer. Within two or three days an opinion was circulated among the nine justices of the Alabama Supreme Court and six of them signed a ruling that stated the veterans home did not need a CON. This was a great victory for us," Faulkner added.

"Although Huntsville was to be a recipient of a home, they were not apparently as nearly interested as Bay Minette in obtaining one, and did not give much assistance, although they did make some effort.

"The original plan was for only one hundred beds but I suggested to Mr. Green that we ask for one hundred and fifty beds, which were eventually built.

"Also, fortunately for Bay Minette, the state eventually came up with some money and we did not have to put up any local funds to obtain the fine William F. Green Veterans Home, which is beautiful and renders a great service.

"The local home has run into some difficulties from time to time because of the shortage of nurses. There has always been a waiting list for veterans wanting to get into this very fine home.

"During the fight to obtain the nursing home, our state representative, Steve McMillan, and Mayor Rickey Rhodes did everything they could to be helpful. Without the solid cooperation from many people, the home would not have been built in Bay Minette," Faulkner concludes.

Index

Acknowledgments

MY DEEP APPRECIATION to my wife, Cameron, whose encouragement and support were invaluable in the completion of this project. And my grateful thanks to longtime editor friend Steve Mitchell for his assistance and thoughtful suggestions in the preparation of the manuscript.

About the Author

ELVIN L. STANTON draws from a wide range of successes in broadcasting, journalism and politics. He is a native of Baldwin County, Alabama, and was born in a small farm home in the Rosinton community near the town of Robertsdale. He was the youngest of nine children, five boys and four girls, of Richard Marvin and Fannie Viola Stanton.

He was a high school teenager when he began his broadcasting career after winning a radio announcers' contest at WHEP in Foley, Alabama. He worked there before and after school and his boss talked him into attending the University of Alabama where he majored in radio and television. While on campus, he worked part-time for the downtown Tuscaloosa radio station, WJRD, and later as the station's news director. He then volunteered for the Army and was an honor graduate of the US Army Information School in Fort Slocumb, N.Y. He remained at the school as a senior instructor of broadcast journalism for the remainder of his tour of duty.

After his discharge from the military, Stanton worked as a journalist for United Press International and was a member of the

Capitol Press Corps during the John Patterson administration. He also covered the arrival of the Freedom Riders in Montgomery, as well as other civil rights conflicts. In the mid-sixties, he became news director of WSGN in Birmingham where he won numerous awards for outstanding news coverage for such activities as the Selma March and the bombing of Sixteenth Street Baptist Church where four young girls were killed.

In the late 1960s, Stanton became general manager of Jimmy Faulkner's two Bay Minette radio stations, WBCA and WWSM. It was there that he originated a political program for candidate George C. Wallace in the contentious 1970 governor's race. Following Wallace's victory, Stanton was asked to join the Wallace administration as assistant press secretary. He later was named press secretary and was involved in two national political campaigns (including the 1972 campaign when Wallace was shot) and two other statewide campaigns for governor. He served as manager of Wallace's 1982 successful gubernatorial campaign and was Wallace's Executive Secretary (chief of staff) during his last administration as governor. Stanton served Wallace continuously for 26 years, longer than any other staff member, remaining with the governor until they both retired from state service.

Stanton has had the opportunity to observe Jimmy Faulkner through the eyes of a journalist, an employee, a political ally, a mentor and a friend for more than four decades.